From Kingdom…

To nigger-dom!!!

From Kingdom…

To nigger-dom!!!

"A People Lost In Translation"

By: Charles E. Dickerson

Neo Nexus Publishing, LLC

NeoNexusPublishing@Gmail.com

COLUMBIA, SOUTH CAROLINA

*

ISBN-10: 0-9846673-7-7

ISBN-13: 978-0-9846673-7-6

Library of Congress Control Number: 2016920081

*

Second Edition

*

PRINTED IN THE UNITED STATES OF AMERICA.

Reference Sources:

Ancient Wisdom.com

Encyclopedia Britannica

Wikipedia Encyclopedia

Merriam-Webster Dictionary

United States Census Bureau

Online Etymology Dictionary

New King James Version

Ava DuVernay
Documentary "13th"

NAACP
Criminal Justice Fact Sheet

Teachers.net Gazette
December 2005, Vol 2, No 12

United States Constitution
13th Amendment, Sections 1 & 2

The Los Angeles Times
November 14, 2012 - By Danielle Ryan

Thirteen/WNET New York
Educational Broadcasting Corporation
"Slavery and the Making of America"

WWW-Virtual Library: History
Map History / History of Cartography: The Gateway to the Subject

Ferris State University (FSU)
Jim Crow Museum of Racist Memorabilia

Emory University - Voyages Database
The Trans-Atlantic Slave Trade

Dr. Henry Louis Gates, Jr.
The African Americans: Many Rivers To Cross

Dr. Yosef Ben Jochannan
Black Man of the Nile and his Family

Dr. Neil A. Frankel
The Atlantic Slave Trade And Slavery In America

Courtesy of The African American Registry
Dr. David Pilgrim and Phil Middleton
"Nigger (The Word), A Brief History"

John G. Jackson
Introduction to African Civilization

Library of Congress
Prints & Photos, Online Catalog

George G. M. James
Stolen Legacy

Lord Baron Raglan
How Came Civilization

Ra Un Nefer Amen
Metu Neter, Volume 1

Robert K. G. Temple
The Sirius Mystery

Malcolm X
"Message to the Grassroots"

Lerone Bennett, Jr.
Before The Mayflower: A History of Black America 1619-1964

AlterNet: Adam Hudson
"1 Black Man Is Killed Every 28 Hours by Police or Vigilantes: America Is Perpetually at War with Its Own People"

Gomes Eannes de Azurara
The Chronicle of the Discovery and Conquest of Guinea

~ Dedication ~

To all of the burnt faces of the world, past and present. *"Burnt Face"* was a colloquial term used by the ancient Greeks to describe and identify people of color during the *"old world"* era, when Africans reigned as Kings, Queens, and Pharaohs.

This book is dedicated to the *"Burnt Faces"* of the modern world whose ancestors endured slavery, oppression, abject poverty, cruelty, and abuse due to their ethnicity and the color of their skin.
We salute you!

~ *Aethi Ops* ~

Contents

Contents

Contents

Contents

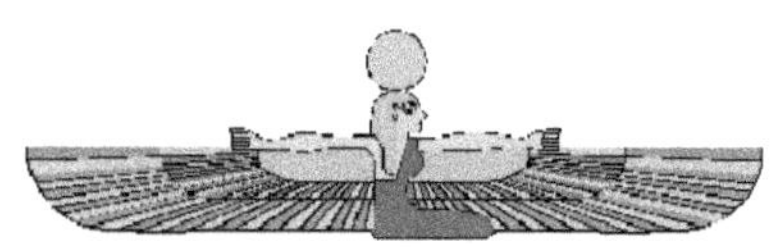

"The Visitation"

Under the guise of *"discovery"* the *"Takers of Mankind"* came... and the *"Havers of Humanity"* welcomed them in unaware. Only later would the descendants of those whom had everything realize their grave misfortune after ending up with practically nothing. The eyes of the world watched in amazement as it stared upon the faces of the once glorious, triumphant, extremely wealthy, and sovereign people of the old world, whom for millenniums had mutually coexisted in the lands of antiquity, only to become known as the *"Have-Nots"*.

The *"Takers"* came in waves upon ships bearing the name *"Jesus"* with banners announcing their *"alleged Christian Faith"*. Immediately upon arrival they began to *systematically kill, steal,* and *destroy*. In an effort to justify their relentless raping, pillaging, and plundering of the many highly civilized and remote nations and cultures of the dark world, the *"Takers"* used the hyperbole of social science to make it appear proper, fitting, and just. The *"Takers"* disguised their concerted sanctimonious actions under the socially conceived, pseudo-scientific banner known to all as...

"SURVIVAL OF THE FITTEST."

This radical departure of anti-spiritual adaptation and cultural denunciation against the *"sister nations of humanity"* marked the end of an era in high culture, which sprang forth from the various seats of remote antiquity throughout the *"ancient world"*.

It is for this reason that we the *"Have-Nots"* of today seek the *"humanitarian virtues"* that our forefathers once shared and embraced prior to *"the visitation"*. Our virtues of *"spiritual morality"* are yet to be rediscovered, duly grasped, and fully understood.

The Admonishment…

"The thief cometh not,
but for to steal, and to kill,
and to destroy…"

~ John Chapter 10, verse 10 ~
King James Holy Bible

~ African… To Africans ~

Our Story… Part One!!!

We are African descendants, irrespective of educational achievement, economic class, social background, skin complexion, genetic characteristics, same or racially mixed parentage, diverse cultural upbringing or place of birth. In effect, we are all Africans at our roots, regardless of our diversity. I am certain that many of you may disagree, but African we are, based upon our place of beginning. This is true regardless of our differences; we are all interrelated in a human family composed of complex distinctions, similarities, and long-lost ties.

The connection is true for all by-way of our genetic heritage and historical linkages to Africa's past; it all began in the *"Motherland"*. When we fail to acknowledge the roots of our genetic heritage *"mankind"* will continue to deny the historical contributions made by those whom are African by natural birth and relatively recent cultural extension.

It is a very sad commentary on human relations to read western history text books that expound on the diverse accomplishments of mankind that lends so little credit to the numerous contributions and achievements of Africans and those of recent African descent. It is upon this basis that the native African and the story of its descendants have inherited the age-old myth, characterizing us as a *"know nothing"*, *"done nothing"*, *"contributing nothing"* race of people.

The African Story... The Story of stories!!!

In truth, the African Story is a very precious legacy of humanity, representing itself as a timeless gift to the world. The African story is a ***"<u>Story of</u>***

stories" untold, deserving to be recognized as surrogate and midwife to all of humanities' stories. The African American story is but a footnote and mere extension of the African story, yet it is loudly crying out for daily and worldly acknowledgment.

Upon being linked, the two stories become a united voice of legacy issuing from ancient Ethiopia's and Egypt's past that speaks beyond the shallow boundaries that makeup the celebratory framework for the *"Total Black Experience"* during the Month of February. *When the two stories are connected, they accentuate the African historical journey, creating an ongoing narrative issuing from both the native Africans and Blacks, honoring the collective achievements of Africans and their American descendants past and present.*

Human history can be interpreted as a story of one's journey and relationship with one's self and others in humanity, relative to the material world that surrounds them. Therefore, human history when broken down is a story in two parts. The first part deals with the journey on the basis of achievement and discovery. The second part deals with the interrelationship of a people on the basis of expansion and recovery.

Therefore, everyone's story is the account of their history, so let's take a look at the characteristics of history. Everything that has a beginning has a history. History is not isolated from who we are or what we do. History casts a light on where we have been and what we have done. History is totally integrated into the human existence and the overall fabric of life. History knows all, sees all, hears all and tells all.

In fact, history is a tool of appraisal that serves as a qualifier and disqualifier in every area of life. History is the oldest and most honest storyteller in existence. History is very similar to people, barring one major exception. If history is not muzzled, shackled or suppressed it does naturally what people do out of prejudice, envy and spite. History unlike people will always give a truthful, detailed and accurate account of past events.

History is an impartial and uninvited guest that eavesdrops and holds nothing back. History when left uninterrupted to function naturally will always tell the truth. History is indeed the biggest and baddest blabbermouth and tattletale on the planet.

When it comes to the African story, history has a lot to say, but not enough time to say it, considering the length of our historical journey going back to our beginning. Our history is *"Our Blabbermouth"*, which has been muzzled and stifled, due to no fault of our own. Finally the time has come for *"Our Blabbermouth"* to speak openly and freely about us, which brings us to the subject and limitations of Black History Month.

Black History Month... An abbreviated narrative!!!

Black History Month is dedicated to the celebration of our journey, wherein the largest and best part has been erased, leaving us with the knowledge of a very difficult *"post-traumatic slavery experience"*. It is important to understand that history is a story of relationship. Imagine not talking candidly to your parents, spouses, sisters, brothers, friends, and acquaintances *only 28 to 29 days out of the year!!!*

This is very important when the *"other ethnic groups"* in America are talking *"collectively"* among themselves, about themselves, and others including African Americans every day of the year.

So how did Black History Month come about? Black History Month had its beginning with Dr. Carter G. Woodson, a noted African-American historian, author, journalist and founder of the *"Association for the Study of African American Life and History"*, in addition to establishing *"Negro History Week"* in 1926. Then in 1970 a group of Black students enrolled at Kent University expanded *"Negro History Week"* into *"Black History Month"*. The selection of February is an irony, simply because African American history being an extension of African history is in fact a major part of the longest historical record of human achievement and accomplishment on the planet. Yet Black history is celebrated during the shortest month of the year with little to no mention of Mother Africa. By reason of necessity and basic understanding Black History should be conjoined with native African history, going back to the commencement of the Trans-Atlantic Slave Trade, wherein the two are celebrated and discussed as one throughout the year.

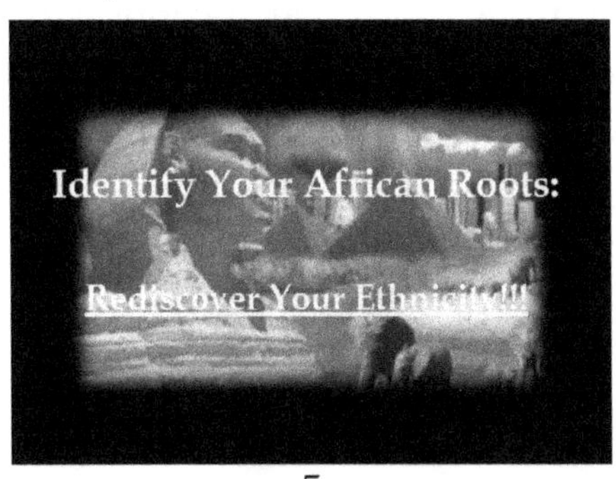
Identify Your African Roots:

Africa... The "birth mother" and tree trunk of nations!

Upon revisiting the *"Family Tree"* of man at its beginning, Africa is viewed as the *"tree trunk of nations"*, prior to the emergence of *"mankind"*. This period dates back to the earliest lineage of man, prior to branches of man evolving from the trunk of the family tree, commonly known as *"humanity"*. *For centuries "mankind" has been at war with "humanity"!!!*

After a very prolonged and undetermined period of time the supercontinent *"Pangaea"* broke apart forming the six sub-continents that exist today. ***Europe is not a continent independent of itself..., see "Eurasia"!!!*** The breakup resulted in individual branches of *"mankind"* emerging, resulting from migratory adaptation to new geographical climates and regions. The intercontinental separation of *"Pangaea" (the Motherland)* produced the secondary branches of man which would become *"mankind"*, only for them to branch-off from the native trunk. The branches became individualized and independent of the trunk itself, only to turn inward upon the elderly trunk many millenniums later, thereby wrapping it up and this is where we the Africans find ourselves today.

Upon examining the life experiences of Blacks in America beginning with the inception of European colonial slavery, research reveals Black history as the dead limb broken off from the African Family Tree, representing the worst part of the *"human story"* and the *"African-African American experience"*.

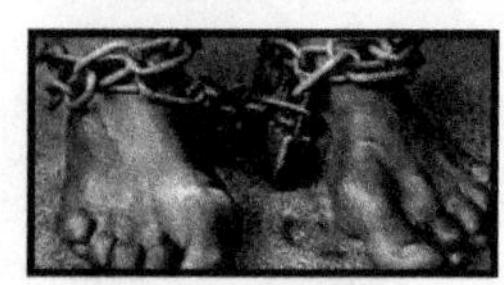

The ownership of a people's story is their most valuable asset aside from human life itself, wherein the story of Black People in America needs to be reconnected to its cultural root, which is indeed Mother Africa. This body of work represents an off-the-cuff chat between ourselves to talk about issues that are vital and important to us.

African History... Part One of the Black Story!!!

Our story is a timeless and endless romance composed of many ancient and institutional legacies that when spoken of in accuracy and truth, cries out loudly in the voices of our ancient African, Ethiopian and Egyptian ancestors, proclaiming the birth and establishment of civilization...

Our story the *"AFRICAN STORY"* was originally conceived, lived and played out in the hearts, minds and spirit souls of our common ancestry for millenniums going back for countless generations into the prehistoric realm of the *"Fraternity of the Wild"*. It is here that the vestiges of our forefathers are linked together in early, primitive existence.

African history is the ever unfolding account of the *"open suppression"* of the worldwide accomplishments and contributions marked by Africans and their descendants throughout the world concerning the authorship, establishment and furtherance of civilization past and present. The *"African Story"* is not a mere fable struggling to be recounted as truth, only fitting to be revisited by African Americans for 28 to 29 days during the shortest month of the year, wherein the word *"Africa"* is rarely if ever mentioned. *Africa is the foundation!!!*

Great African names such as Osiris, Isis, Horus, Imhotep, Anhkenaton, Ramesses, Thutmosis, King Tut, Hannibal, Hapshuset, Nefertiti, Chaka Zulu, Patrice Lumumba, Toussaint L'Ouverture and countless others would ring out from among the pages of western history books like bells, chimes and tingling cymbals, if the *"human story"* was accurately and honestly told.

For example, Imhotep was the very first Renaissance man in recorded history. He was the world's first known architect who is credited with building Egypt's first pyramid known as the *"step pyramid"*. Imhotep is recognized by many noted scholars, Egyptologist and historians as the world's very first physician. He was also a priest, scribe, sage, poet, astrologer, vizier and chief minister to King Djoser, the Egyptian Pharaoh of the Third Dynasty who reigned from 2630 B.C. thru 2611 B.C..

Unfortunately, like countless others, Imhotep's name and accomplishments are not recorded in any western history academic text books. This race of people about which I speak preceded the Athenians, Greeks, Romans, British, Europeans and Americans by tens of thousands of years. In ancient times the African continent and her people were known as *"Ethiopia"* and *"Ethiopians"*, in addition to the southern part of the Atlantic Ocean being named the Æthiopic Ocean. History credits the Ethiopians with creating and developing the basic building blocks and institutional components of civilization.

From the earliest times we find undeniable and irrefutable proof of Ham, *"Father of the Africans"* and his descendants, the Ethiopians being the authors of *agriculture, algebra, architecture, astronomy, time keeping, mathematics, geometry, literature, government, medicine, metallurgy, masonry, engineering, painting, religion, sculpturing, science and papyrus, which is the earliest form of paper.* They also invented the *art of writing* and authored the oldest known books of *"Wisdom Literature"*, commonly referred to as *"The Teachings of Ptahhotep"* and the oldest book of worship known as *"The Book of the Dead" a.k.a. "Coming Forth by Day"*.

The African people pioneered the Earth's very first

governmental system, that if properly acknowledged would be referred to as the "FIRST FAMILY OF THE EARTH". Our ancestors worshipped the stars, romanced the heavens and reverenced the Earth. *Over centuries and millenniums they became the initiating and founding fathers of the institutions of art, astrology, numerology, mathematics, writing, law, philosophy, science, medicine and masonry.*

The *"Ethiopians"* aka *"Burnt Faces"* are direct descendant of the Biblical Ham *(pronounced Kem in the native tongue)* who is recorded as the second son of Noah in the Old Testament Hebrew text of the biblical Genesis. The Egyptians were the architects and builders of the magnificent sphinx, pyramids of Giza and the great pyramid, which is the only surviving edifice of the Seven Wonders of the ancient world.

Thousands of years prior to the voyage of Christopher Columbus the Egyptians had already crossed over the Atlantic Ocean onto the American shores after having sailed up and down the River Nile for millenniums in awe inspiring grace and splendor.

We have scientific and archeological proof of this based upon the findings of nicotine in the hair follicles of King Rameses' The Great's 3,000 year old mummy. In addition, to the distinct commonalities of architectural and design technics that are present in both the Egyptian pyramids of Giza and the pyramids located in South America. *It is worth noting that the tobacco plant is native to the American Continent* and it was not grown in other parts of the world during the time and reign of King Rameses, the Great.

The biblical record of Ethiopian historical lineage!!!

During Old Testament times biblical characters such as Pharaoh, King Solomon, Moses, Moses' sister Miriam, Moses' nephew Aaron were all *"Burnt Faces"*, indicating the influence of *"melanin"* on the entire Hebrew lineage going back to and preceding the biblical patriarch Abraham... who is referred to as *"The Father of Faith"* and *"The Father of Many Nations"* in the Old Testament Canon of the Hebrew Bible.

As a matter of fact, King Solomon *(son of King David)* stated the following about himself... *"I am black, but comely" (Solomon 1:5)*. There is also the record of God turning Moses' hand white *(Exodus 4:6-7)* and his sister Miriam completely white *(Numbers 12:10)*. In addition, the following is recorded about Jesus in the book of Daniel chapter 7, verse 9 *"...And the hair of His head was like pure wool."* Also in the book of Revelations chapter 1, verse 15 this is recorded... *"... and His feet like unto fine brass, as though they burned in a furnace"*. Now I can't speak for you, but this sounds a lot like a brother wearing an afro and sandals to me!

Ethios Ops... Face of the melanin connection!!!

Prior to the emergence of the European nation states the following list of nations were all recognized as part of the Ethiopian or Burnt Faced family of nations: *Kamit (Ancient Egypt), Sumer, Babylon, Canaan, Elam, Kush (Ethiopia), Indus Kush (India/Eastern*

Ethiopia) and the Harappa Valley civilization. This well-kept secret can only be understood on the basis of the Greek inspired name *"Ethiopian"* that is equivalent to the term *"Black"*, which was adopted by African Americans and used for identification since the 1960s.

The African *(Ethiopian)* contribution to the development of the ancient world and new world is irrefutable and undeniably staggering. The well documented, though hidden facts of who we are and what we have accomplished is yet to be recognized and realized, *especially by our own people*, which flies square in the face of the myth that characterizes the African and its Black descendants as a *"know nothing"*, *"done nothing"*, *"contributing nothing"* race of people.

History has irrefutable proof that Africans are the *"original kingdom builders"* dating back to the Great Flood!!! There is scientific DNA evidence and genetic research dating back to early antiquity proving Africans are the people from whom the subgroups of mankind evolved and later learned from.

African legacy stolen & "Civilization" plagiarized!!!

So it is on this basis that we share the wealth of a very timeless and untold story. A story that spans the complete course of human existence, having been played, down-played, recorded, re-recorded, plagiarized and subverted down through the ages. The African story is a timeless and endless romance between man, God and nature. The African story started out as an uninterrupted fairy-tale with kingdoms, empires and dynasties of kings, queens, priest-kings and pharaohs who descended from ancient generations of people of color that existed prior to recorded history that are far too numerous to count.

This story is indeed the African story, celebrating a history that precedes, overlaps and engulfs western history to an extent unimaginable by today's historical, technological and cultural standards. The Four Institutional Pillars that support the platform of civilization in modern society evolved from our ancient ancestors, which are *Religion, Philosophy, Medicine and the Arts & Sciences*.

According to George G.M. James, noted author and Black historian, the Greeks acquired their earlier knowledge of high culture and civilization from Egyptian priests through tutorship and later from the Library of Alexandria in Egypt following the conquest of Egypt by the Persians and Alexander the Great, wherein Aristotle, Plato, Socrates and Hippocrates were later dubbed... *The Fathers of Religion, Philosophy, Medicine and the Arts & Sciences*.

> *"After nearly five thousand years of prohibition against the Greeks, they were permitted to enter Egypt for the purpose of their education. First through the Persian invasion and secondly through the invasion of Alexander the Great.*
>
> *From the sixth century B.C. therefore to the death of Aristotle (322 B.C.) the Greeks made the best of their chance to learn all they could about Egyptian culture; most students received instructions directly from the Egyptian Priests, but after the invasion by Alexander The Great, the Royal temples and libraries were plundered and pillaged, and Aristotle's school converted*

> *the library at Alexander into a research centre. There is no wonder then, that the production of the unusually large number of books ascribed to Aristotle has proved a physical impossibility, for any single man within a life time." {Page 1... "Stolen Legacy"}*

Jim Fournier, information technologist and co-founder of Planetwork recorded the following concerning the source of Greek knowledge...

> *"It follows that the ancient Greeks should be taken at their word when they claim that their knowledge is of great antiquity and was derived from Egyptian sources.*
>
> *Indeed it is nothing if not bizarre that modern scholars of the Greek world should go to great lengths to dismiss such claims on the part of the authors of the primary texts themselves, to instead rely on the advice of modern Egyptologists that the ancient Egyptians had no such knowledge." {Planetworkers.org}*

Lord Baron Raglan, a British historian and author recorded the following definition of civilization...

> *"A society is civilized only if it contains scholars and scientists. The scholar consolidates and clarifies the knowledge that has been acquired and passes it on to the scientist, who engages in experimentation to increase the knowledge. Without the torch of learning the scientist is reduced to groping in the dark and the scientist is not able to use and test the results, causing the scholar to drown in obscurity.*

Thus scholarship and science are the bedrock and foundation of civilization. Both the scientist and the scholar are dependent upon the written word. The written word enables the scientist to use the learning of the scholar, who must have the ability to record the results of his investigations. Civilization depends upon scholarship and science, which depend upon writing. Therefore, civilization can only arise where the art of writing is known." [Paraphrased quote from pages 3 & 4… "How Came Civilization?"]

Ra Un Nefer Amen, a noted Panamanian historian and author recorded the following concerning ancient Black nations and their contributions to the establishment of civilization…

"Now we can understand why, for example, all the fundamental skills and institutions of civilization began with Black nations (Kamit [Ancient Egypt], Sumer, Babylon, Elam, the Harappa Valley civilization, Kush [Ethiopia], Indus Kush [Black India], and Canaan).

Because of their people's ability to learn from intuit, 6000 + years ago, the knowledge that forms the basis of our civilization (religion, mathematics, geometry, medicine, astronomy, writing, literature, agriculture, metallurgy, government, architecture, painting, sculpturing, algebra, science, etc.)." [Quote from Metu Neter, Volume 1, pages 7 – 8]

Our story, the Ethiopian and African story can be summed up in one word...

"CIVILIZATION"!!!

Europeans and the Trans-Atlantic Slave Trade!!!

Unfortunately, European enslavement of Africans emerged in the Middle Ages with its aligned cadre and crew of modern scholars, Egyptologist and supporting cast of lying historians that went about the business of systematically *distorting, erasing and plagiarizing* the historical record of African achievement. This historic fabrication served the purpose of *"mentally enslaving"* the African captives by taking away the *"knowledge of self"*. This was done for the purpose of fortifying the Trans-Atlantic Slave Trade, which had its birth in 1444 A.D. in Lagos, Portugal, wherein 235 Africans were kidnapped to be sold as slaves in 1441 A.D. by Prince Henry, son of King John 1 contradicting the centuries of lies stating that the European enslavement of Africans began with Africans voluntarily selling their people to the Europeans.

In fact, the Atlantic Slave Trade, which morphed into the Trans-Atlantic Slave Trade, did not begin with Africa selling her people into European enslavement. Thanks to Napoleon Bonaparte's candidness on his view of history and truth, the foundation of European History was openly exposed to the world for all people of color to see…

"History is a set of lies agreed upon."

Therefore, we must take Emperor and conqueror, Napoleon Bonaparte *(1769 A.D. - 1821 A.D.)*, General and Commander of the French Army at his word, when going about the business of validating our history, based upon the *"statement of facts"* presented regarding the non-achievement of Africans and Blacks.

Diligent research has proven that Western history is an intentionally biased, watered down, distorted version of accomplishments and achievements by *"people of color"* that conveniently portray Black people and other people of color in the darkest light. The White man's version of our story is *"His"-story...*

"Humanity's commonality is rooted in "Blackness!!!"

In fact, the incomprehensible greatness of Egypt and the key role that she played in the establishment of civilization caused panic among countless European historians, scholars and writers, who went to great lengths to disconnect her from any ties with the Ethiopian and African people by claiming that Egypt was located in Asia and not on the African continent. Western history books documented this for centuries.

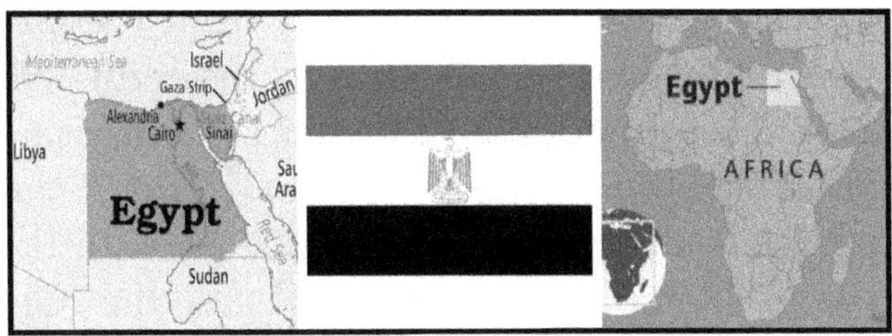

Subsequently, the White scientific community and European historians from around the world have tried their best to cover up the ground breaking truth that ancient Egyptians were African and Black. The cover up was exposed based upon recent disclosures on the part of respected modern scholars and archeologists in the historical community, whom validated the obvious that Egypt is in fact located on the African continent, thereby discrediting the European *"statement of fact"* that the Egyptian pharaohs <u>were not</u> of Ethiopian and Nubian origin and descent.

The following is recorded in *"Physiognomonica in Histories"*, which was written by the ancient Greek philosopher Aristotle... *"the Ethiopians an Egyptians are very black."* Also, the following is recorded in *"The Histories, Book II"*, which was written by the ancient Greek historian Herodotus... *"because like the Egyptians they had black skin and wooly hair."*

During ancient times our ancestors were commonly referred to as Ethiopians, properly defined as *"Burnt Faces"* by the Greeks, whom authored the name. In the original Greek language the definition of *"ethios"* is *"burnt"* and the definition of *"ops"* is *"face"*. Upon combining the two terms, the *"melanin infused Africans of old"* and their *"dark skinned descendants"* inherited the description of *"Burnt Faced"*.

The term *"Ethiopian"* originated from the Greeks and was equivalent in meaning to the term *"Black"* that was recently adopted by African Americans in the mid-20th century. The 20th century term *"Black"* is appropriately descriptive and consistent with the 9th century B.C. term of *"ethios-ops"* as the Greeks originally applied it in their day.

During the ancient era of Old Testament times the term *"Ethiopian"* was descriptive of all people of color regardless of their ethnic grouping, geographical location, or nationality in the same way the term

"Coco Gene" is used by the Japanese and Okinawan's today, when referring to a person displaying melanin *("the genetic tanning agent")* in his or her skin.

As a matter of fact, what was true during the time of the Greeks is still true today, relative to the presence of melanin in one's skin, *or lack thereof!!!*

The term *"Ethiopian"* in its original formulation was applied to the indigenous people that originated in the heartland of Africa formerly known as *"Alkebulan"*. These are those with whom the Greeks engaged in social intercourse through regional trade practices in Egypt and the neighboring countries abroad. The understanding of this one crucial fact is central to the question of...

> *"What is the true identity of the people that bore the label "Ethiopian", being referenced biblically and historically, beginning with the Greeks and continuing until this day?"*

Melanin... The hereditary code of racial identity!!!

To better understand the significance of the question of Ethiopian identity, relative to the world's viewpoint of African ancestral identity, we need only look to the way that the term *"Caucasian"* applies to the *Englishman born in Britain and living in Bermuda, Canada, Grenada, or Istanbul,* the person is identified as *"Caucasian"*, *due to the lack of "melanin" in his or her skin*.

If the *Swedish, Scandinavian, or Polish is living and breeding in America, Thailand, South Africa, Bolivia, or the Andes,* he is identified as *"Caucasian"*, simply because his body lacks the *"melanin"* needed to produce *"hue"*, thus rendering him *"White"* by racial classification.

During a very early period in ancient history the term *"Ethiopian"* applied to the native Africans exclusively. Only later would its racial implications negatively affect other people of African lineage on the basis of color, *due to the presence of melanin in one's skin, regardless of ethnic grouping or nationality originating from the Greek word "melas", which refers to "dark brown and black pigment in the skin"*. This truth is evidenced by the ethnic title *"Eastern Ethiopians"* that was conferred upon the ancient people of India by the Greeks, only for them to be colonized by Britain millenniums later beginning in 1757 A.D. to 1947 A.D..

The "human family" which includes "mankind"...

... predominate made-up is composed of people of color!!!

During the post-colonial and post-slavery period all people of African descent receives varying degrees of *"burnt faced treatment"* by Europeans worldwide relative to their native ethnicity and country of origin in the aftermath of the implementation of *"Race"*.

The opposite is true for White People, wherein the term *"Caucasian"* is applied to Europeans and their descendants worldwide regardless of their ethnic grouping or nationality, *based upon the lack of melanin in their skin*. If the *Frenchman* is born in *Paris* and lives in *Yugoslavia, Ireland, Somali or Afghanistan,* he is classified and referred to as *Caucasian.* If the *Englishman, Dutchman or German is living and breeding in Russia, India, Iraq, Arabia, or the Amazons,* they are still considered *Caucasian* for the simple reason that they originated from the Caucasus Mountains and their skin lacks melanin and color, causing them to appear white.

So why aren't the *Ancient Egyptians, Sumerians, Babylonians, Canaanites, Elamites, Kushites and Eastern Indians* identified *"Ethiopian"* based upon the presence of melanin in their skin, relative to white people that are identified *"Caucasians"* due to the lack of melanin in their skin? I would venture to say that *"ethios" "ops"* which signifies *"burnt faced"* based upon the presence of melanin in one's skin should also apply to the *Aborigines, Native Americans and Ancient biblical Hebrews (including Jesus)* by-way of human lineage and hereditary extension arising out of the Motherland.

I consider this to be true on the basis that all people of color originated from those whom are historically classified as *"Burnt Faced"*. I consider this to be appropriate and fitting on the same basis that all *"white faced"* Europeans are classified as *"Caucasian"*.

According to the Greek definition of Ethiopian that is derived from *"ethios ops", "ethios" meaning "burnt" and "ops" meaning "face" ("burnt faced"),* all people that possess melanin in their skin should be classified as *"Burnt Faced"* on the same basis that all *"Caucasians"* are classified *"White"* due to their *"white faces"*. All people of color the world over who are *"Burnt Faces"* have made tremendous contributions to the world's cultural and technological advancements issuing from their ancient *"Ethiopian" - "Burnt Faced"* ancestry.

In fact, since the beginning of human creation the human family was labeled *"humanity"* based upon inclusion of all people on the planet vs. exclusion. Up until the 16th century the word *"humanity"* was used *"collectively" to label the "global family" prior to the advent and introduction of "race"*. Race was devised to separate and divide people of color from white people. There is only one race... which is the *"Human Race"* that is composed of many kindred's and tribes!!!

The earliest classification for the *"family of man"* issues from the word *"hue"* that lends itself to color, going back to the name of the first human... *"Adam"*. The name *"Adam"* signifies color based upon the color of the *"clay of the earth"* from which Adam was created.

"Hue" signifies color based upon the presence of *"melanin"* in the skin, which functions as a *"biological tanning agent and youth preservative"* in people of color, thus engendering an old adage among Blacks that says... *"Good black don't crack"*. Melanin has served as a *"hereditary code of genetic identification"* for people of color since the beginning of human history going back to the original humans at the beginning of time.

> *"Adam" is both the proper name of the first human and a designation for humankind. God himself gave this appellation to Adam and Eve (Gen 5:1-2). The color red lies behind the Hebrew root adam [; 'a]. This may reflect the red soil from which he was made.*
>
> *Adam was formed from the ground (Gen. 2:7). Word play between "Adam" and "ground" (adama [h'm'd}a]) is unmistakable. It is important that Adam is identified with humankind rather than any particular nationality. The country from which the dust was taken is not specified. Rabbis believed it came from all over the earth so no one could say, "My father is greater than yours." (www.biblestudytools.com)*

So once again I ask the question… why is it that the *Ancient Egyptians, Sumerians, Babylonians, Canaanites, Elamites, Kushites and Eastern Indians, including the Aborigines, Native Americans and Ancient Hebrews (including Jesus)* all being people of color are not historically classified as *"Burnt Faced"* on the same basis that all white faced Europeans are classified as *"Caucasian"*? The answer is quite simple… the root of this question is directly linked to the establishment of European colonization and a global slave commodity, namely… *the African and their direct descendants!!!*

Introduction of "Race" creates division in man!!!

Prior to the 16th century and the birth of the Trans-Atlantic Slave Trade the word *"race"* did not apply to people, but to competitions, pedigrees of wine, etc..

This is extremely significant for all people of color who represent the overwhelming majority of the human family!!!

The following is recorded in the Etymology Dictionary regarding the origin of *"race" as it applies to people…*

> *"Original senses in English included "wines with characteristic flavor" (1520), "group of people with common occupation" (c. 1500), and "generation" (1540s)."*
>
> *"people of common descent," a word from the 16th century, from Middle French race, earlier razza "race, breed, lineage, family" (16c.), possibly from Italian razza, of unknown origin (cognate with Spanish and Portuguese raza)."*
>
> *"Etymologists say no connection with Latin radix "root," though they admit this might have influenced the "tribe, nation" sense.*
>
> *Meaning "tribe, nation, or people regarded as of common stock" is by 1560s."*
>
> *"Modern meaning of "one of the great divisions of mankind based on physical peculiarities" is from 1774 (though as OED*

points out, even among anthropologists there never has been an accepted classification of these)." {Etymology Dictionary - race (n.2)}

Hereditary isolation and fractured racial identity!!!

By disabling the *"hereditary code of genetic identification"* that linked all people of color together through *"melanin"* and replacing it with *"race"*, the social apparatus by which collective labeling was naturally established was systematically dismantled, resulting in a multi-cultural disconnect that would give rise to the establishment of *"Isolated Regional Identities"* throughout the world, resulting in *"Race"* morphing into *"Racism"* around the globe beginning with the dehumanizing method of European enslavement that was inflicted upon the Africans.

Melanin serves as a *"common linkage"* and *"ethnic identifier"* pointing back to the Motherland as its source. Unfortunately, melanin in today's world serves as a badge of rejection for those whom are blessed to possess it. *According to Professor and historian John G. Jackson, those lacking melanin during ancient times were looked upon as "sickly" or "cursed by God" for not having been blessed by the rays of the Sun during the era of sun worship. The curse of leprosy was similar in biblical times, because it depleted the melanin in one's skin. (*See Leviticus chapter 13:9-13... "The entire body & hair of ancient Hebrews turned permanently & completely white".)*

The application of *"Isolated Regional Identities"* became common place and within centuries was cemented into the global landscape and human relations practices of the Europeans slavers and colonizers. The practice was instituted and reinforced around the world in the lives of people of color by way of geographical lines being drawn, signifying national and tribal borders that resulted in *"boundaries based upon race"* that were tailored to the geography of the lands in which they lived, producing racial division known as *"hereditary isolation effect"*.

The *"hereditary isolation effect"* that resulted from the practice of division and separation caused all people of color to be identified based upon *"geographical groupings"*, rather than the presence of melanin in their skin, which was passed down biologically as a natural inheritance from Adam, the first human. *The "authentic human" is a person of color*.

This in effect, divided ethnic groups within the *"human family"* one from another along tribal lines within their collective cultural lineage, thereby producing a global proliferation of *"fractured racial identities"*. This would lead to the diminishing and in some cases a complete loss of native ethnicity.

> *Ethnicity... "a category of people who identify with each other based upon similarities, such as common ancestral, language, social, cultural or national experiences. A groups ethnicity is characterized by ancestry, history, homeland, language, dialect, religion, mythology, ritual, food preparation, style of dress, art, physical appearance, and shared cultural heritage."*

Western history is riddled with cases where people of color bound by common ancestry shared a wide variety of phenotypical groupings that when labeled in isolation would form the *"racially prescribed mical regions of the world"*. The lines that were drawn to form the territorial boundaries on the new world maps that formed the territories of European colonization have shifted back and forth over the centuries, due to political gerrymandering and wars between the European colonial invaders. The Treaty of Versailles serves as proof of this undertaking…

> *"One of the chief contributing causes of the Second World War was the Treaty of Versailles (June, 1919), that officially ended the First World War. Its main terms were surrender of ALL German colonies in Africa and the Far East, which would be mandated to Britain, France, Belgium, South Africa, Japan and Australia. This led to a re-distribution under a series of mandates." {GeneralHistory.com}*

History has shown when there is a breakdown in the collective elements of large family groupings in a society; such an event marks the beginning of the loss of *"native ethnicity"* and the dismantling of *"CULTURE" that can be attributed to the introduction of "race"!!!*

The impetus for this early latent practice was rooted in the emergence of Greece coming out of the Dark Ages about 3,000 years ago *(1100 B.C. – 700 B.C.)*. Under the influence of Egyptian tutorage Greece would become prominent in the Arts and Sciences, thereby establishing herself as a civilized nation-state. Her rise can be attributed to the knowledge acquired from the tutorship of Egyptian priest and all out pilfering from the Library of Alexandria located in Alexandria, Egypt several centuries later. As a result Greece would come to be regarded as the foundation of European cultural influence and seat of intellectual power in the ancient and modern world.

The undermining of Egyptian and African culture began by Greece's claim of being the "SEAT OF CIVILIZATION". This move would reposition and elevate Greece into a place of prominence and notable acceptance, whereby she falsely laid claim to the title and cultural status of being the *"originator of civilized knowledge and higher learning"* of the ancient world. Greece's false claim went into effect in the aftermath of the fall of the Egyptian Empire and pharaonic culture that had existed for 3,000 plus years under the rule of royal Egyptian dynasties going back to 3100 B.C..

The absorption of Egyptian idealism into Roman culture in 30 B.C. by way of the Greeks positioned Europe as the world's center of *"thought and power"* positioning Europeans as the soon to be recognized *"MASTER RACE"* 1600 years later. Rome would inherit the stolen legacies of Ancient Africa and Egypt from Greece only to couple them with ruthless military power to the furtherance of Europe as a rival power and intellectual base from which Europe would challenge and control the lands of antiquity around the world leading up to the present day.

The evidence of this has been observed and recorded over the past three millenniums with the emergence of Greece as the *"cultural seat"* of European Power. As a result, the sister nations of antiquity that are identified as third-world nations today were prominent Nation States during the age of antiquity, prior to becoming remnants of the ancient cultures of the world. It is here that we find the ancient cultures of the old world having been dominated militarily and geographically remapped to weaken widespread targeted areas of ethnic concentration. This was done by adding, redrawing and moving long established borders to divide, dominate, control and conquer the darker populations of the world that were living and existing under constant terror and unrelenting seize.

Upon comparing maps of the new world to those of the old world, we find global redistricting and large scale gerrymandering beginning in 1492 A.D. with the Spaniard's inauguration of the *"Age of Discovery" aka "Age of Exploration"*. This was the beginning point of ancient nations, cultures, and lands being massacred, dominated, plundered, stolen, remapped, and destroyed by multiple nations of European invaders.

The biblical résumés of Noah's three sons!!!

To better understand how the world has changed since the time of the ancients, due to *"European cultural domination"* and *"ethnic reclassification"* of people of color, Blacks have come to be known as a *"know nothing", "contributing nothing", "accomplishing nothing"* race of people. Yet this appraisal does not square with the oldest historical record of African people that is found in the Bible, when read from a "*résumé perspective*" versus a "*genealogical perspective*".

The following biblical account provides a geographical description of the Earth's reconstruction and its rebuilders in the aftermath of the great flood:

> *"Genesis chapter 10, verses 6 thru 20 describes the descendants of Ham as being located in*

North Africa, Central Africa and in parts of southern Asia".

Upon researching the Scriptures for references to Africa, the descendants of Ham and her kindred nations, Ethiopia and Egypt are noted in the Bible more than any other countries of the world that are mentioned in Scripture.

Ethiopia is biblically known as *Cush* and *Egypt* is biblically known as *Mizraim*. The name *Cush* is translated *Ethiopia and Mizraim* is translated *Egypt*. *Cush* and *Mizraim* are the first and second *sons of Ham*, the father and progenitor of the African Race.

The Bible sets forth a biblical account in the book of Genesis chapter 10, verses 1 thru 32, wherein the résumés of Noah's three sons provide evidence of the contributions of their individual achievements toward the rebuilding and restoration of the world that was laid barren by the waters of the Great Flood.

It is very important to note that God designated dual assignments for Noah and his three sons. Noah's assignment began prior to the flood with the building of the ark, based upon building specifications provided by God. After completing the building of the ark Noah was charged with inventorying all of the animals and bringing them aboard the ark in the numbers and order specified by God. The last phase of Noah's assignment was to bring willing members of man aboard the ark with the goal of saving the *"human family"* and all of the earthly creatures that would otherwise have been destroyed by the flood.

According to the biblical account, Noah's family

was chosen by God to start the world over and Noah now 600 years of age had three sons who were to be the builders. *Shem, Ham* and *Japheth* are their names. Shem the elder would become father of the *Jewish nation*, *Ham* the second son would become father of the *African nation* and Japheth the youngest son would become father of the *European and Oriental nations.*

The assignment of the three sons of Noah was entirely different than their father's. The Bible provides individual résumés detailing the accomplishments of each of the three sons after the ark landed on Mount Ararat and the flood waters were abated. The assignment given to Shem, Ham and Japheth began once the voyage had concluded.

Even though the biblical text does not reference an assignment being given to Noah's sons, we can conclude that Shem, Ham and Japheth were charged with rebuilding the kingdoms of the Earth in the aftermath of the Great Flood. This is especially notable in light of the fact that Noah was more than 600 years of age at this given point in time.

As a matter of fact, there is no notable mention of Noah in Scripture after this point and time, barring him making wine and physically exposing himself while passed out and intoxicated. Noah's behavior was his way of signifying that his unprecedented and overwhelming assignment had been completed.

The following biblical account provides details of the résumés and accomplishments of Noah's three sons. The résumé of Nimrod notes the ***"beginning of accomplishments"*** by Ham's descendants rebuilding the world versus Shem and Japheth, wherein there is no biblical record of accomplishment for them during the resettlement period in the aftermath of the flood…

- ***Japheth's Résumé*** - To whom a total of four scriptural verses, *2 thru 5* are allocated detailing the children born unto him *without any mention of greatness, kingdoms, constructed cities, or accomplishments,* only to be identified as the coastland peoples of the Gentiles that were separated into their lands according to their languages, families, and nations.
- ***Shem's Résumé*** - To whom a total of eleven scriptural verses, *21 thru 31* are allocated detailing the children born unto him *without any mention of greatness, kingdoms, constructed cities, or accomplishments,* noting only that he had offsprings and that their families moved to Mesha as you go toward Sephar, the mountain of the East.
- ***Ham's Résumé*** – To whom a total of fifteen scriptural verses, *6 thru 20* are allocated detailing the beginning of the rebuilding of the world beginning with Ham's grandson Nimrod. The text also provides the genealogy of Ham and the regions they settled into surrounding the resting place of the ark *(*Probable lands of resettlement that were domiciled by Ham's descendants prior to the flood)*. The sons of Ham were *Cush (Ethiopia), Mizraim (Egypt), Phut (Lybia), and Canaan (Palestine).*

"6 The sons of Ham were Cush, Mizraim, Put, and Canaan. 7 The sons of Cush were Seba, Havilah, Sabtah, Raamah, and Sabtechah; and

the sons of Raamah were Sheba and Dedan.

"[8] Cush begot Nimrod; he began to be a mighty one on the earth. [9] He was a mighty hunter before the LORD; therefore it is said, "Like Nimrod the mighty hunter before the LORD."

Note: It is here that we have clear evidence of the beginning of the rebuilding of the world with Ham's grandson Nimrod and Nimrod's relationship with God…

[10] And the beginning of his kingdom was ***Babel, Erech, Accad,*** *and* ***Calneh,*** *in the* ***land of Shinar.*** *[11] From that land he went to Assyria and built* ***Nineveh, Rehoboth Ir, Calah,*** *[12] and* ***Resen*** *between Nineveh and Calah (that is the principal city).*

[13] Mizraim begot Ludim, Anamim, Lehabim, Naphtuhim, [14] Pathrusim, and Casluhim (from whom came the Philistines and Caphtorim). [15] Canaan begot Sidon his firstborn, and Heth; [16] the Jebusite, the Amorite, and the Girgashite; [17] the Hivite, the Arkite, and the Sinite; [18] the Arvadite, the Zemarite, and the Hamathite. Afterward the families of the Canaanites were dispersed.

[19] And the border of the Canaanites was from ***Sidon*** *as you go toward* ***Gerar,*** *as far as* ***Gaza;*** *then as you go toward* ***Sodom, Gomorrah, Admah,*** *and* ***Zeboiim,*** *as far as* ***Lasha.***

[20] These were the sons of Ham, according to their families, according to their languages, in their lands and in their nations."

African knowledge versus the European narrative!!!

In addition to the sons of Ham initiating the rebuilding of the old world, Mizraim *(Egypt)* the 2nd son of Ham determined the accurate length of the calendar year. This was accomplished by the Egyptians counting the number of days between the star Sirius *(*Sothis" in the Egyptian language)* appearing in the sky from one cycle to the next coinciding with the annual overflow of the Nile River.

Once every 365 days the Star Sirius would appear in the sky and shortly thereafter the sun would peak over the horizon and then the Nile River would overflow. The Egyptians counted the days between the Star Sirius rising and the Nile River overflowing from one cycle to the next, resulting in the accurate calculation of the 365 day year and the solar calendar.

At this exact point in time, the Roman calendar consisted of 10 months totaling 295 days, with 2 floating months known as *"intercalary months"* being attached. During its entire use, Roman timekeeping was referred to as the *"Years of Confusion"* and the *"Clash of Calendars"*, wherein the planting seasons did not coincide with the solar calendar causing ongoing agricultural chaos and economic confusion.

The Roman Emperor, Julius Caesar learned of the Egyptian's 365 day calendar from Queen Cleopatra following the Roman conquest of Egypt in 47 B.C., which resulted in the hiring of an Egyptian astronomer by the name of *"Sosigenes"* in 46 B.C.. Sosigenes reconstructed Rome's defunct calendar into 12 sequential months, doing away with the *"two intercalary months"* and the contemporary Roman calendar became the Julian calendar.

In October 1582 A.D. the Gregorian calendar was introduced, being named after the Roman Catholic Priest, Pope Gregory XIII, wherein an additional ¼ day was added each year for four years producing Leap Year and February's 29th day of the month.

In the aftermath of the calendar's reconstruction, one of the original months was shortened from 30 days to 28 days, allowing for two other months to be renamed and lengthened. One of the months gained an additional day and was renamed July after Julius Caesar and the other month gained an additional day and was renamed August after Julius' great nephew, Augustus Caesar making both months 31 days.

As a matter of record, the calendar that Sosigenes reconstructed was initially composed of seven 30 day months and five 31 day months, equaling 365 days in the year. For the record, there were no 28 or 29 day months in the calendar that was created by Sosigenes.

In fact the 2nd month was originally a 30 day month until the Roman Emperors Julius Caesar and Augustus Caesar decided that they each would take away one day from the month which would become February, wherein they both being emperors felt that they were royally entitled to have one of the longest months of the year named after them. The loss of 2 days resulted in February becoming the shortest month of the year versus the 30 day month that it was initially.

The only exception is Leap Year, which occurs every four years based upon the Gregorian Calendar which adds 6 hours annually, resulting in February becoming a 29 day month once every four years, thus constituting a completed 4 year cycle equaling 1461 days and 16 seasons.

The ancient knowledge of the star *"Sirius A"* and its companion dwarf star *"Sirius B"* was known for thousands of years prior to the Europeans by the Egyptians who determined the 365 day year in addition to a rather primitive tribe of West Africans, known as *"the Dogon People"*.

The term *"Dog Star"* and *"Dog Days"* are directly linked to the *"Dogon People"*, whom possessed this ancient knowledge as early as 3200 B.C. resulting in the star Sirius being referred to as the *"Dog Star"* from whence comes the saying... *"dog days of summer"*.

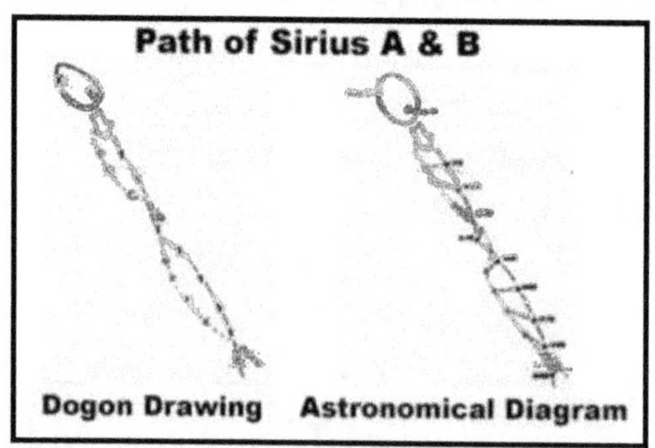

The Dogon Tribe has celebrated the 50 years orbital cycle of the dwarf star *"Sirius B"* orbiting *"Sirius A"* in ritual ceremony every half century going back 3600 years prior to the invention of the first recorded *"heavenly observable telescope"* by Galileo Galilei.

Galileo Galilei

1564 A.D. thru 1642 A.D.

Galileo Galilei was an *Italian astronomer, physicist, mathematician, philosopher and inventor* credited with inventing the first recorded telescope capable of observing heavenly bodies that were not visible to the naked eye. Prior to Galileo's discovery of the modern telescope in 1610 A.D., such knowledge was considered impossible by the Europeans, *when considering the fact that "Sirius B" is not visible to the naked eye.*

The Egyptian's knowledge of the Star Sirius was known for thousands of years prior to the arrival of the Greeks and Romans. The Egyptians also possessed the knowledge of the *"precession of the equinoxes"* that could only be calculated through human observation during it entire duration to determine its length, requiring the knowledge of the 25,920 years orbital cycle to be determined by-way of human observation. This knowledge was known to the Egyptians millenniums prior to the invention of Galileo's telescope, which credits the Egyptians with having a known existence that goes into the past well in excess of 30,000 years, constituting a time period that is inconceivable by European time keeping and historical standards.

European scientist and scholars are baffled by both the Egyptians' and Dogon People's awareness of such knowledge, which cannot be explained and does not fit into the European narrative of a *"know nothing"*, *"done nothing"*, *"accomplished nothing"* race of people.

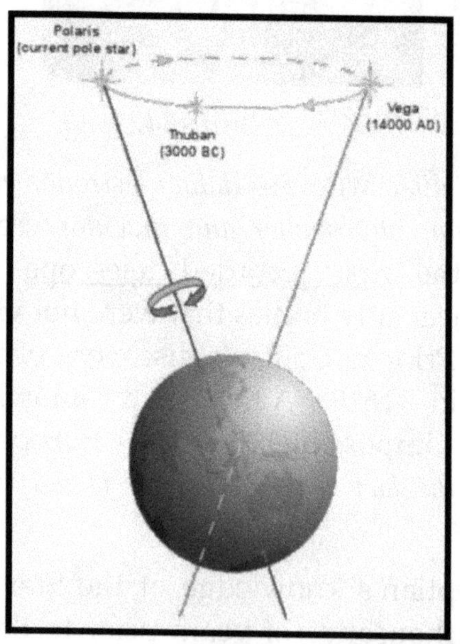

"The precession of the equinoxes is the observable phenomena of the heavenly constellations appearing to slowly rotate around the northern hemisphere of the Earth."

"Each constellation taking turns at rising behind the rising sun on the vernal equinox as the Earth's axis completes a full cycle of rotation taking approximately 25,920 years."

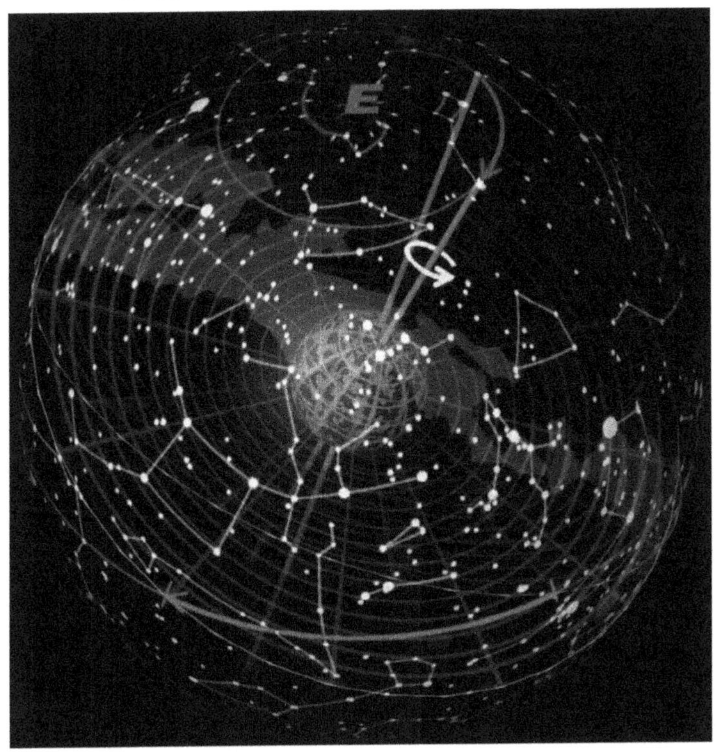

"This remarkable cycle is due to a synchronicity between the speed of the earth's rotation around the sun, and the speed of rotation of our galaxy." {Ancient Wisdom.com}

African mega achievements validated in Scripture!!!

The African story includes many staggering accounts such as these that need to be told, especially to our own people. In fact, everything that we have been told about the lack of accomplishment among our people is a lie. The Bible serves as an additional source of validation revealing an entirely different story than what we have been told, based upon dated and recorded information going back to the great flood.

If the truth was accurately and honestly told the descendants of Ham, were the *"true kingdom builders of humanity"* going back to the great flood, while his brothers Shem *(father of the Jews)* and Japheth *(father of the Europeans)* simply got off of the ark, made babies and left. Unfortunately, the European Nations of Japheth, in whom the Bible has no record of achievement or accomplishment returned centuries later as *"takers"* to rob the descendants of Ham out of what their forefathers had foundered and built. The Bible also records the descendants of Japheth encroaching upon the habitats of Shem *(Gen. 9:27)* when they *("ancient Hebrews_Israelites")* were engaged in recording the Old Testament Canon of the Bible.

To better understand the African story, it is important to have an in-depth knowledge of where we the African people come from and who we were as a people, prior to the arrival of the European conquerors in the Motherland and the ensuing Trans-Atlantic Slave Trade that followed. Africa was not the original name of the Motherland; various names were applied to the continent going back into ancient times, leading up to the present. The African label was applied to the continent by the Romans thousands of years later.

The native name for Africa was *"Alkebulan" (mother of "humanity" and "mankind")*, wherein we referred to ourselves in our native tongue as the *"Children of*

Alkebu". This name was used by the *Moors, Nubians, Numidians, Khart-Haddans aka Carthaginians and Ethiopians.* Africa was also called *Kemet, Libya, Ortegia, Corphye, Egypt, Ethiopia, Sedan, Olympia, Hesperia, Oceania and Ta-Merry.*

The same is true for the native name of the father of the African people, which was translated into other tongues causing it to be pronounced and spelled differently at different points in time. The native pronunciation of *"Egypt"* or *"Mizram"* is *"Kem"* for *"black land"*, but is pronounced *"Kam"* and biblically recorded as *"Ham"*, coinciding with the entire African continent having once been named Egypt with Kem.

> *"Psalm chapters 105, verse 23 mentions the "Land of Ham" in Egypt and Psalm chapter 78, verse 51connects the "tents of Ham" with Egypt." "In Genesis chapter 10, Nimrod, son of Cush (whose name means "black") founded a civilization in Mesopotamia." "In Genesis chapter 11, God calls Abraham out of the land Ur of Chaldees, whose earliest inhabitants included blacks."*

As a Christian I find it discouraging that the following excerpt was printed in a copy of the *"NIV Bible Companion Dictionary"* that has been in my possession for years. Unfortunely, this dictionary could still be in circulation today, influencing the minds of many. This is another example of *"alternative facts"*, *"false narratives"* and *"lies"* that are taken directly out of the 15th and 16th century playbook of Europeans slavers, who for centuries have gone about the business of discrediting Africans and Blacks…

~ *NIV Bible Companion Dictionary* ~

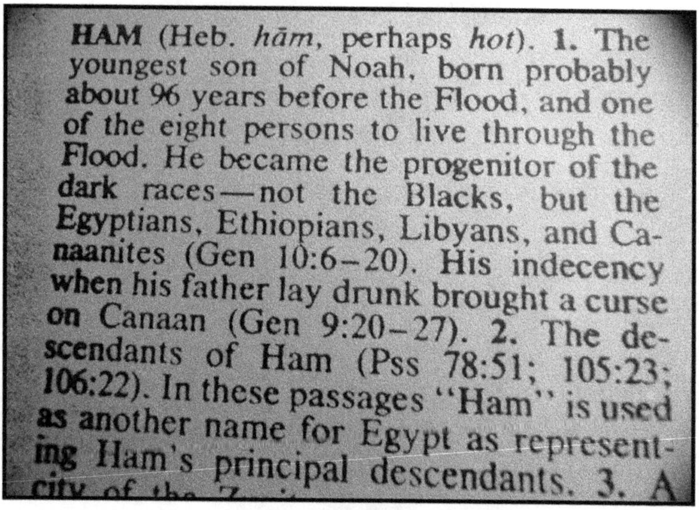

HAM (Heb. *hām*, perhaps *hot*). **1.** The youngest son of Noah, born probably about 96 years before the Flood, and one of the eight persons to live through the Flood. He became the progenitor of the dark races—not the Blacks, but the Egyptians, Ethiopians, Libyans, and Canaanites (Gen 10:6–20). His indecency when his father lay drunk brought a curse on Canaan (Gen 9:20–27). **2.** The descendants of Ham (Pss 78:51; 105:23; 106:22). In these passages "Ham" is used as another name for Egypt as representing Ham's principal descendants. **3.** A city of the

~ *Extracted Excerpt* ~

> *"Ham, the youngest son of Noah, born probably about 96 years before the Flood, and one of the 8 persons to live through the Flood. He became the progenitor of the dark races -* ***not the Blacks****, but the Egyptians, Ethiopians, Libyans, & Canaanites (Gen 10:6 -20)".*

This is just another disturbing example of how far the Europeans and their descendants will go to discredit Africans and Blacks on the world stage.

So the question is... If Blacks are not descendants of any of Noah's three sons, *where did we come from? Did we fall out of the sky? Were we brought here by aliens? Were we hatched by some strange oceanic creature?* Or maybe, they are saying... *we really don't exist!!!*

For centuries the Europeans whom hijacked Christianity during the time of the Romans and never truly understood it, have used the Holy Bible as a weapon and tool of subversion to subjugate and arrest the minds of African people and people of color in the face of mistruths and racial aggressions for the furtherance of their white nationalist agenda. When a people's ideology trumps their faith, their politics is truly their religion!!!

African history, legacy and truth!!!

As a dedicated disciple of Christ for 45 years and one devoted to the study of the Holy Scriptures, I believe it totally fitting and proper to use the biblical account of Noah's three sons to set the record and true identity of the Africans straight regarding their contribution to the world. This is a vital step towards resurrecting the *cultural esteem*, *ethnic esteem* and *personal esteem* that is so critically needed for people of African descent, individually and collectively.

I believe it vitally important to reiterate the statement made by Napoleon Bonaparte…

"History is a set of lies agreed upon."

This statement sums up a great deal of Western History, especially as it pertains to people of African descent who have been fed a steady diet of lies and untruths beginning with the Greek conquest of Egypt in 332 B.C. by Alexander the Great, which culminated in the 15th & 16th century with the European's establishment of the Trans-Atlantic Slave Trade, *wherein they, the "White Nations" mutually agreed and colluded to enslave and brainwash Africans indefinitely*.

It is critically important to note that *"History is the guardian of legacy for a people who have their survival and destiny at hand."* We are in fact those people!!! We are the people that have been victimized and devastated by the untruths that have left us ill-equipped to defend or feel worthy of ourselves as a group. African history spans the breadth and depth of the *"Black Experience"* with a watchful eye focused on legacy.

Legacy has to its credit the fixed origin and ownership of its initiates, whom authored the processes of *"nation building"* and *"civilization"* with the sole purpose of passing the acquired knowledge and benefits down to their heirs.

It is impossible to take back that which has been lost to the past, but we have an obligation to future generations to take back "OUR TRUTH", that being the story of our experience, which is... The Black Experience!!! We also have the awesome duty of learning the total truth about ourselves. The "TRUTH OF ONE'S SELF" is that one irrevocable commodity in life that equips one to be free.

There are three indelible truths... "*personal truth*", "*collective truth*" and "*Divine Truth*". Truth is the voice of *"Total Experience"* issuing from the past.

The knowledge of one's total experience is their *personal truth,* which is known only to the subjects of such truth. The knowledge of a group's total experience is its *collective truth,* which is known only to its people.

The knowledge of the total experience of "CREATION" from the beginning of time until the end is the *Divine Truth,* which is known only to the Omniscient God and Creator of the Universe.

Personal truth is reflected upon and uttered by the beholder of such truth, collective truth is spoken by the oracles of its people and the Divine Truth is spoken and recorded by the prophets of God. Our résumé and our story come with biblical credentials having the *"Word of God" as our "Truthful" and "Divine Witness".*

In our current state, we are strikingly similar to keys with holes in our heads that are longing to be filled with the knowledge of ourselves that can only be derived from our native ethnicity, thereby ensuring the much needed success that we are lacking collectively as a people to unify us competitively as a formidable ethnic group.

When left unfilled we are void of the knowledge of our natural potential for greatness, making us susceptible to being clipped on and off the *"keychain of American slave culture"*. Due to the lack of self-knowledge, we are doomed to failure, versus the success shared by other ethnic groups in America.

It is impossible to clip a "key" back onto a "keychain"…

When the hole in its head has been filled with its natural properties!!!

Without the *"knowledge of self"*, we are ill-equipped as a group to *challenge success* in the *economic, political, educational and corporate arenas of American life.* Self-knowledge creates the collective cohesion that is needed to compete with the *"immigrant ethnic groups"* that arrived in America fully arrayed with their native cultural armor and knowledge of self fully intact.

Our inability to defend and advance ourselves collectively is evidenced by the ongoing police killings, criminalization, mass incarceration, political manipulation and economic disenfranchisement that have left us to fend for ourselves without the transformative knowledge needed to bring about the changes that are necessary. The time has come for us to collectively embrace our "Cultural Truth" by rediscovering our "Native Ethnicity" and "True Heritage"!!!

We would be wise to heed the prophetic warmings issued by the prophet Hosea and the Apostle John...

"My people are destroyed...
for lack of knowledge..."
Hosea 4:6

"And You shall know the truth, and the
Truth shall make you free"
John 8:32

Study to know your collective truth...
and the knowledge of your native ethnicity
will transform you and make you free!!!

~ Dawn of European Slavery ~

His-Story… Part Two!!!

History provides written record of a large number of Africans being kidnapped by the Portuguese in 1441 A.D. and taken to Portugal as slaves to be auctioned off to other Europeans. This maiden event marked the beginning of what would ultimately become the Trans-Atlantic Slave Trade and the forged inception of the Black race into the Americas.

In 1441 A.D. Prince Henry *(3rd son of Portugal's King John 1)* initiated the first major European slaving expedition by sending six ships to West Africa under the command of Lançarote de Freitas, the Revenue Officer of Lagos. All of the ships were fitted with banners that read *"Order of Christ"*. The journey is recorded in *"The Chronicles of the Discovery and Conquest of Guinea"*, by its author Gomes Eanes de Azurara. Gomes Eanes de Azurara describes the Portuguese capture of 235 Africans that took place in the present day West African land of Mauritania.

> *"We saw the Moors with their women and children coming out of their huts as fast as they could, when they caught sight of their enemy. Our men, crying out St James, St George and Portugal, fell upon them killing and taking all they could.*
>
> *There you might have seen mothers catch up with their children, husbands, their wives, each one trying to flee as best he could. Some plunged into the sea, others thought to hide themselves in the corners of their hovels, others hid their children underneath the shrubs that grew about there, where our men found them." "And the Moors of that capture were in number 235."*

{The Chronicles of the Discovery and Conquest of Guinea, 1896-1899 - Chapter 24}

According to Azurara, the Portuguese raiders attacked several other villages returning with no less than 235 captives. All were taken to Lagos, Portugal where on August 8, 1444 they were marched to a meadow on the outskirts of town where the first European slave auction was held. Reportedly, Gomes Eanes de Azurara was there and was terribly moved by the treatment of the Guinea captives.

In the year 1445 A.D. Prince Henry established the first European slave market and fort in Arguin Bay, Lagos for the purpose of auctioning the kidnapped Africans into slavery that had been forcefully acquired beginning four years earlier. It is here that the Atlantic Slave Trade began. Prince Henry's introduction of *"Portuguese slave raiding"* would later morph into *"systematically coerced trans-Atlantic slave trading"* throughout the North American hemisphere.

Just a couple of centuries later on Bunce Island in Sierra Leone and other parts of western Africa,

Africans were trading Africans to Europeans in the thousands for guns, liquor, money, fine apparel and other commodities. According to Dr. Henry Louis Gates, Jr. over half of the African captives that were forced into slavery were sold by Africans during the course of the Trans-Atlantic Slave Trade.

The Trans-Atlantic Slave Trade was a *"European initiated commercial enterprise"* that was foundered upon the *supremacy of power, merciless and ruthless attacks, domination, violence and coercion,* only for it to evolve into a mutual partnership with the less militarized West Africans that lasted until the end of the American Civil War. What began as a Portuguese inspired, coerced business venture would later escalate into all-out human poaching, village raids and systematic kidnappings by European and African headhunters, who began to view all West Africans as a human source of potential wealth. It is important to note that tribal wars resulting in the selling of the captured from defeated tribes fueled the birth of homegrown slavery in Africa long before the Trans-Atlantic Slave Trade began.

THE GRAPHIC
THE AFRICAN SLAVE-TRADE—SLAVES TAKEN FROM A DHOW CAPTURED BY H.M.S. "UNDINE"

Africans of all ages, genders, trades and vocations were captured, marched, dragged and hauled aboard the awaiting slave ships that docked in the various ports of entry to load their human cargo. Fleets of ships were draped with *"banners of Christ"*, including one in particular that was named after Jesus. These ships were later crammed and stuffed beyond capacity with African captives from all walks of life before embarking upon the 8 to 10 months voyages that crisscrossed the Atlantic Ocean to reach *"Europe"* and the *"New World"*.

"16th Century Slave Cargo Ship"

"Jesus of Lübeck"

"Jesus of Lübeck became involved in the Trans-Atlantic slave trade under John Hawkins, who organized four voyages to West Africa and the West Indies between 1562 and 1568.

During the last voyage, Jesus, along with several other English ships, encountered a Spanish fleet off San Juan de Ulúa *(modern day*

Vera Cruz, Mexico) in September 1568.

In the resulting battle, Jesus was captured by Spanish forces. The heavily damaged ship was later sold for 601 ducats to a local merchant." {Wikipedia Encyclopedia}

Africans of all backgrounds and classifications were *hunted, herded, stolen, branded and traded* by professed Christians of European religious persuasion before being sold individually and in mixed groups *(small and large)* to the European and American slave merchants, whom auctioned them off to the *"rich and soon to be wealthy landowners"* in Europe and the barren lands and islands in the Americas.

Data retrieved from the shipping logs of *Voyages: The Trans-Atlantic Slave Trade Database* provides records of 12,521,336 captives being transported into the Americas *(1501 A.D. - 1866 A.D.)*, including 305,326 that entered into North America *(1619 A.D. - 1865 A.D.)*. For 246 years African slaves were treated as *"sub-humans"* and trade-labelled *"niggers"*. *Dreadfully, tens of millions more were kidnapped, smuggled, and pirated, whom perished and have gone undocumented!!!*

It is here among the millions of Africans issuing out of *lost religions, customs, tongues and tribes* that the trans-Atlantic slavery story took root and flourished in the mining camps, sugarcane groves, tobacco lands and plantations in the West Indies, Europe, North America, South America and Central America.

The dreaded Africans boarded the slave ships as deposed village kings, queens, tribal chiefs, priests, doctors, artists, artisans, musicians, farmers, spinners, weavers, herdsmen, tradesmen, among various other craftsmen and laborers, only to be cast to the bottom of the social, economic and human rungs of European, American and Caribbean societies, where a large number of Blacks find themselves today.

This is a book of cultural ambivalence that has been written and compiled for the ones of us that have been lost in cultural translation, seeking an explanation to how our own people could have sold us into slavery. It also begs an answer to how the Europeans that *kidnapped, stole* and *forced-purchased us* could have subjected us to an *"unprecedented institutional system of abuse"* and *"nigger-dom"* that erased our ethnicity with the intent of paralyzing our human growth and quarantining us in a state of cultural ignorance that would forever bind us to a system of free labor.

Unfortunately, our loss of ethnicity rendered us equivalent to a *"bouquet of roses"* in comparison to the Europeans and Asians that migrated to North America with their cultural roots intact. The flourishing of their native ethnicity and culture is evident in the American economy emanating from the cultural ingredients and recipes of their native ethnicity. We on the other hand were stripped of our cultural identity upon being forged into a foreign land and profoundly racist culture without the freedom and cultural tools to properly translate and assimilate as migrant citizens. The slaves were transfixed in a distorted space and skewed time, due to the severing of their cultural roots of ethnicity. The results engendered the most horrific form of slavery inflicted upon a people in the entire history of man.

To better understand the *"prescribed damage"* that was done due to the lack of knowledge concerning our *"native culture"*, we need only compare a *"rosebush"* that is planted in the ground to a *"bouquet of roses"* that is deposited in a vase *without a root*. Upon comparing the two it is apparent that a rosebush that is rooted will outlive the planter. Unlike a bouquet of roses that cannot survive without a root, thus causing it to wither and die. The rosebush being rooted allows it to draw the essential life sustaining nutrients from its native soil, versus a bouquet that is artificially confined in a container that is similar in function to a *"plantation"*, thus depriving it of the vital nutrients that are necessary for it to adapt, flourish and grow.

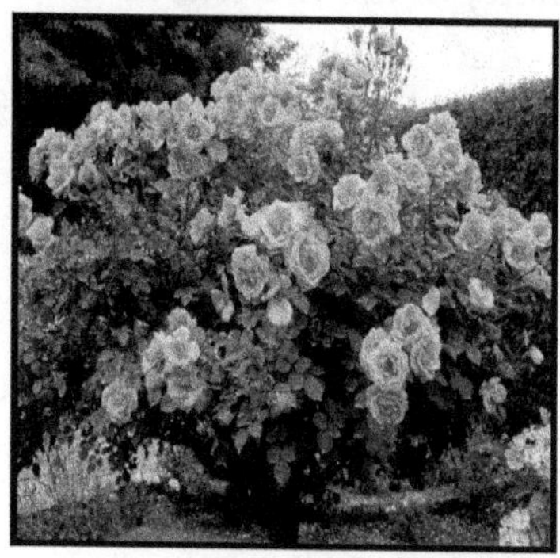

Without root the bouquet blooms but never blossoms, whereby each individual stem is forced to rely solely upon itself, thus guaranteeing a futile existence. The bouquet survives for a very brief period as a group of individual stems, but never survives as a collective unit to bloom, blossom and reproduce generationally over and over and over again, perpetually. The stems of the bouquet strives separated, being individually supported by the vase because there is no root to nourish, strengthen and support the stems collectively, thus rendering the bouquet the most vulnerable of any plant on Earth. The bouquet lives for a short period of time being separated into individual parts of a whole before it withers and dies for lack of nourishment, requiring constant care prior to being replaced in a newly recurring cycle that begins again and again at zero.

Worst of all... the bouquet has to start over from scratch after each and every passing generation and when placed alongside the *"ethnic rose bushes of the world"* that are rooted, unified, resilient and vibrantly strong the bouquet is not ably equipped to collectively compete nor stand. *The bouquet is incapable of regrowing its root due to lack of life, but with dedication to the study of our history we are indeed able!!!*

Fortunately, slavery was abolished on April 9, 1865 in North America when the Confederate Army was defeated by the Union Army, rendering its government, monetary currency and slave-based economy nonexistent. Yet many slaves did not learn of their freedom until months later, on June 19, 1865; this date is traditionally observed by Black Americans as the *"Juneteenth Celebration"*. Unfortunately, the property aspect of slavery transformed the once free Africans into a *"slave commodity"*, wherein the word *"nigger"* would become a *"property brand"* equivalent in magnitude to that of *Google, Apple, Microsoft, Nike, Facebook, Pepsi and Coca Cola,* which is yet to be erased.

Ironically, even though the Africans and their American born descendants were no longer *"legal property"*, the *"property brand"* was permanently affixed to them and continues to be used today as a degrading and *"derogatory racial brand"*, even though the *"chattel property"* status no longer legally exist. Yet Whites continue to engage the so-called *"n"-Word* to denote *"derogatory branding"* and Blacks embrace it as an *"endearing cultural marker"*, wherein both are ignorant of the fact that it was a *"commercial property brand"* denoting a *"geographical place of origin"* in the West African interior of *"Niger"*, where innocent fathers, mothers, sisters, brothers, and little children were forcefully extracted, traded, and sold for profit.

The use of the word *"nigger"* by Whites and Blacks represents the continuing vulgar indulgence of the mutually agreed upon arrangement by the early Europeans and Africans who stole, bought and sold *innocent people* into slavery when the Trans-Atlantic Slave Trade began. *This is an irony and a travesty!!!*

Slavery, Property and Nigger!!!

Ethnicity... Erased!!!

*"But many that are first shall be last,
and the last shall be first."*

*A prophetic verse from the first...
Foreshadowing Africa's slavery birth!*

~ *Matthew* 19:30 ~

Since the earliest of times slavery has existed in one form or another, wherein one individual or group have subjected others to forced servitude for the purpose of extracting free labor. The primary motivation for slavery is to rid oneself of the toils of labor by forcing the hideous responsibility upon another without residual cost.

The *Trans-Atlantic Slave Trade* was uniquely different from earlier forms of slavery in that it robbed its subjects of their cultural heritage and ethnic identities. For 444 years the less militarized, less organized, disenfranchised West Africans were exploited by generations of rich and powerful European colonists and corporate investors for the purpose of personal gain and perpetual profit.

More than twenty two generations of West Africans whom were gainful, intelligent, productive, law abiding citizens were reduced to *"property"* and brought to the New World as *"native savages"* and counted *"three-fifths of a man"* in the United States Constitution, *Section 2 - The House (Paragraph 3).*

*The Trans-Atlantic Slave Trade was West African natives of the land of **Nigrita,** being bought and stole, caught and sold, before being traded by their frightened old village chief for apparel and a few bottles of brandy and rum, only for the guilt-ridden chief to be kidnapped and sold into slavery several weeks, months, or years later.*

*The Trans-Atlantic Slave Trade was being born with a slave bounty on your head, because your pregnant African mother gave birth while passing through the land of **Nigro**.*

*The Trans-Atlantic Slave Trade was going for a Sunday walk in the land of **Nigriti,** and months later being sold to the highest bidder at the Old Slave Mart in Charleston, South Carolina. In the mid-1850s slave prices ranged from $100.00 upward to $1450.00 depending upon age, sex, family grouping, physical condition, special skills, and other appraisal criteria.*

*The Trans-Atlantic Slave Trade was going hunting in the forest of **Negro Land,** only to be stalked, poached, trapped, and branded with an "x" on your chest before being sold to an awaiting ship captain headed for the Caribbean.*

*The Trans-Atlantic Slave Trade was being kidnapped from the land of **Nigritie,** before being beaten, branded, and sold into Christian slavery, while receiving the enslaving captain's wholesale blessing of baptism in the name of God the Father, God the Son, and God the Holy Spirit.*

*The Trans-Atlantic Slave Trade was being captured from the land of **Nigritia,** and later auctioned into slavery to work in the rice fields of South Carolina, where according to Dr. Henry Louis Gates Jr. 1/3 of the slaves died from snake bite, and malaria in the first year, and 2/3 of the children were dead before they reached their 16th birthday.*

The Trans-Atlantic Slave Trade was the inability to run

faster than a gazelle, and camouflage yourself better than a leopard, resulting in your ending up in a cage headed for the port of Sierra Leone for shipment to Brazil.

The Trans-Atlantic Slave Trade was husbands, wives, mothers, and babies crying, brothers, sisters, and children dying of self-inflicted wounds rather than becoming slaves.

The Trans-Atlantic Slave Trade was having gashes, cuts, and bruises on your back, an iron mask on your face, and an iron collar around your neck, because you were discovered to be an African tribal warrior upon being captured.

The Trans-Atlantic Slave Trade was being a Black African king, queen, doctor, translator, or priest, only to pass through "The Door Of No Return" in Senegal West Africa with chains on your arms, and shackles on your legs, while in route to the gold mines, sugar, rice, cotton, coffee, and tobacco fields of the Americas to work without pay forever, and never see your family, and homeland again.

These examples are just a mere fraction of the

countless atrocities that took place beginning with and during the Trans-Atlantic Slave Trade, when American Blacks were forged into existence as a ***"separate and distinct race of people, whose cultural heritage and ethnicity was erased".*** The slaves experienced a *"genetic transformation"* stemming from the unwelcomed and unavoidable sexual encounters and abuses that occurred between the slaves' powerful and controlling European slave masters and our helpless African and African American ancestors.

This predominate factor accounts for the wide ranging differences in skin complexions, phenotypes and hues among Blacks that further skew and fracture our collective and individual sense of ethnic identity. The ***"obvious lack of ethnic unity"*** among Black's is basically nonexistent in other ethnic groups that operate on the basis of "COLONY" in America.

> *"Colony... is defined as a community of people of one nationality or ethnic origin that are concentrated in a particular place, foreign country or land, but maintain ties to their native country or homeland." (Originating from the Latin word "colere", which means to "cultivate"...)*

Far too many Blacks embrace the notion that colonization has passed, when in fact all ethnic groups in America operate on the basis of *"self-imposed colony"* except us; colloquially speaking, the saying... ***"Blacks don't stick together"*** is true. Unfortunately, the foundational pillars of *"colony"*, which are *"ethnic unity", "economic independence" and "political power"* that were forged into existence by Jim Crow were alive and well in the Black community prior to July 2, 1964, only to be abandoned gradually for *"ACCESS"* leading to *"integration"* in the overall quest for *"Civil Rights"*.

In America there are two colony groups, a *"Greater Colony Group" and a "Lesser Colony Group"*. The *"Greater Colony Group"* is composed of the various Caucasian ethnic groups that collectively make up the power structure in America. The *"Lesser Colony Group"* is composed of the minority ethnic groups that have migrated here from around the world that band together to ensure their *"ethnic unity", "economic independence" and "political power"* for the sake of common good. Unfortunately, we do not fit into either group from a collective standpoint.

Each of the *"lesser colonies"*, be they Mexican, Jewish, East Indian, Arab, Korean, Chinese, Vietnamese, Japanese, etc., abide by a *"Self-Imposed Colonial Code"* that endows them with the *"ethnic unity", "economic independence" and "political power"* that is necessary for them to move to the *"next level"*.

In this instance we are the exception; *we lack the "cultural knowledge of self" that unifies and strengthens us to make us independent collectively and interdependent upon one another.* Unfortunately, we do not function as a colony and for this reason we continually exhaust the capital resources needed to capitalize on what we are able to do *collectively*. Our African and African American ancestors were extremely *able* and the *"building of America"* is standing proof of that fact.

Unlike the slave masters, they were capable *("cap-able")*, simply because they had the much needed capital to resource the things that our ancestors were able to do... *"for them"*. Where on the other hand, we a bonded and unpaid people were not afforded the freedom or the resources to do the same for *"ourselves"*. In fact, *money, knowledge and freedom* were treated as contraband requiring severe punishment.

As African Americans, our social orientation differs greatly from that of the other ethnic groups that came to America as immigrants of their own free will. Our forced migration into American culture set us apart due to the rigid orientation and anti-social restraints that created the psychological bondage that we the 21st century African Americans are still experiencing today. When it comes to recognizing and realizing the vital importance of embracing the first half and best part of our story, we are indeed suffering from a cultural form of *"PTSD"* that can best be described as *"Post Traumatic Slavery Disorder"*.

Our assimilation into American culture differed greatly from that of our European counterparts in that they were not disconnected from their *history, heritage, language, religion, ancestral bloodline and native culture,* which is their *ethnicity* and *native cultural root*. The colonial immigrants were *"made free"* upon setting foot on American soil and this one critical factor provided the legal credentials for them to be regarded and treated as full blooded Americans. The deeply ingrained *"native cultural properties"* of the immigrants were left undisturbed and firmly intact allowing them to *properly translate* into American culture. In fact, their *"native cultural properties"* were promoted; channeled and nurtured to serve as the *"basic building blocks of the American economy"*, wherein we are the *"number one consumer group"* by choice.

To understand the importance of what I am saying, we need only review our generational group progress relative to the other ethnic groups in America going back 150 years to emancipation and after weighing the collective results, ask the question… WHY?

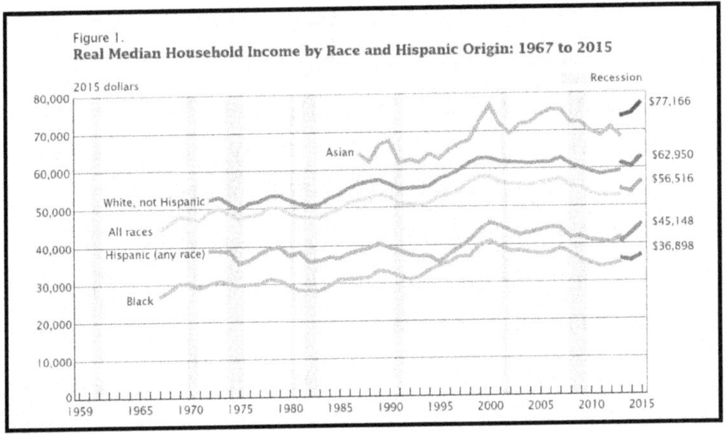

So why do all of the other ethnic groups in America show more positive and progressive signs of ethnic prosperity from generation to generation except us? Why is it that today we can go out and purchase a *British, Japanese, Chinese, German, Italian, French, Swedish, Korean* automobile, but not an *African or African American* automobile? Why is it that today we can go out and purchase *French, Italian, Mexican, Chinese, Japanese, Greek, German,* and many other types of ethnic foods, but in the majority of cities we cannot purchase *African* Food? *We need to take a long pause as a group and ask the question… WHY?*

Why is it that today we can go out and easily buy Italian suits and shoes, French perfumes and the finest Yugoslavian led crystal, but it is hard if at all possible to find an African or African American button to sew onto the French suit, or an African or African American tire to mount onto the German car, or buy an African or African American sock to wear inside the Italian shoe, or purchase an African or African American spoon to eat the Greek food out of the Yugoslavian plate. *We need to take a long pause as a group and ask the question... WHY?*

This reminds me of something that I heard an older African American minister say many, many years ago during a church service in Atlanta, Georgia...

> *"When things aren't going right, we don't need to be told by anyone that there's a dead cat on the line; you just know."*

So when we look around America today and see all of the other ethnic groups moving ahead generationally, while we are being left behind, we shouldn't need to be told that something is wrong, we should automatically know that something is wrong. And the question is... *Is there something wrong with America or is there something wrong with us?*

> *The answer is that there is something wrong with both... but we can't fix whats wrong with America until we fix whats wrong with us!!!*

When it comes to African Americans there is no doubt that something is wrong in America, but the *"wrong in America"* will not change until we invest in the knowledge of ourselves and change the things that are wrong with us.

In essence, African Americans lack the *"cultural knowledge of self"* going back to our native root that is necessary and capable of producing the vital resources that are needed for us to capitalize on what we as a group are able to do for ourselves.

Our African and African American ancestors were extremely able and the *"building of America"* is evidence and standing proof of that fact. Now the slave master on the other hand was *"capable"*, or should I say *"Cap... able"*, because he had the necessary *"capital"* to resource the things that we the Africans and African Americans were *"able"* to do... *"for him"*, while not being afforded the freedom and resource for 246 years to do for *"ourselves"*.

Slavery did a number on Black People. It molded us into the image and likeness of a common key that is designed with a hole in its head that creates a void for the designated purpose of securing and un-securing the key at will. When left unfilled the void leaves African American's open to being clipped off and on the *"key chain of America's slave culture"*.

So the first thing we need to do is to educate ourselves to understand what is meant by... *"moving to the next level"*. We have to rid ourselves of the notion that moving to the next level is an individual process based upon consumption. We have to understand that moving to the next level is not the act of buying a new or newer automobile, purchasing a bigger house, or getting a better job to consume more.

NEXT LEVEL for Black People involves a collective process of transitioning from *"able"* to *"capable"* *(cap-able)* and this is done by learning what we can pour out of ourselves, rather than what we can take in through the process of indebtedness and consumption. More often than not we fall into the *"slavery mentality trap"* of buying into the *"low self-esteem scenario"* by rendering a low appraisal of ourselves based upon the adversary's viewpoint without realizing that the root-word to self-esteem is *"teem"*, which is defined the process of *"pouring out"*.

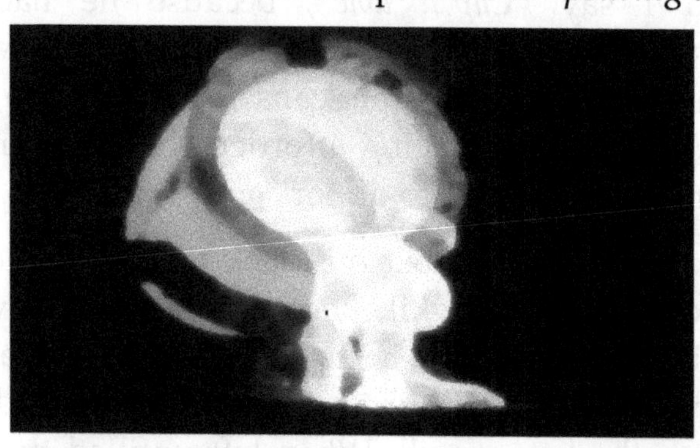

The word *"esteem"* comes from the process of appraisal, based upon estimated *("es")* outpouring *("teem")*. Therefore, it is impossible to *estimate* what we can *pour out of ourselves* until we know and understand that which has been poured into us by our ancestors that came before us.

The appraised value of all things is based upon present condition, relative to the current and historic value of same or like pieces. In short, present and future value is based upon historical value. We the 21st century African Americans are placed in positions on a daily basis wherein we need an accurate appraisal of ourselves to receive fair and equitable treatment and compensation. In these instances we must look deep within ourselves going back to our ancient ancestry during antiquity if needed, in order to determine our individual and collective worth.

*W*e cannot afford to allow others to continue to devaluate our *history, abilities, efforts and contributions* on a daily basis, while chaperoning their histories and performance results to the forefront of life. When allowed, they dictate when and how we are to live and celebrate our *"Journey of Relationship"* with one another. When we allow others to dictate when and how we are to interpret and receive *"our Story"* they take away the good for themselves, leaving us with a *"bad report", "bad position" and a "bad name"!*

*W*e need to reconnect with our *"Total Experience",* which is our *"collective truth",* with the understanding that the largest and best part of our story has been *systematically distorted, plagiarized and erased.* We have a current day example of this with the ongoing and recent effort of overturning the *"Affordable Care Act" and other legislation by President Obama.* This is a continuation of the 8 year mission undertaken by the racist conservative base in the Republican Party to dismantle and erase President Obama's historical legacy, which began on his very first day in office.

*O*ur daily job and individual responsibilities is to take back the legacy of our forefathers that have been stolen by allowing them to come alive again in us and dutifully pass them on to our young. When there is no historical legacy, there is no extension of self!!!

*W*e need to begin to view our complete history and native past as a friend and not an adversary. We have been conditioned to celebrate the worst part of our history, while lacking the realization that our *"Total Experience"* reconnects us to the roots of our heritage and our glorious past. We can no longer afford to allow the psychological trappings of British Colonial Slavery to determine our paths and destiny.

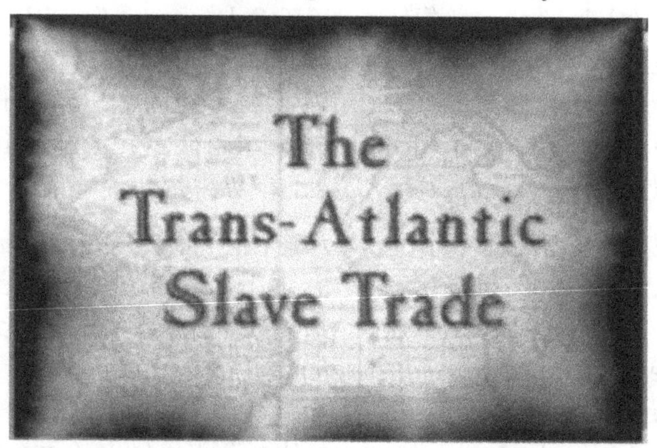

This and more is true, much to the chagrin of Black People who look at things as they are, with little concern or fore-thought being applied to how things use to be. There are many who would rather shut their eyes to the damaging effects of British colonial slavery by imagining the horrors and carnage of the Trans-Atlantic Slave Trade never happened.

We seriously need to examine ourselves in light of our fears and denial and then reach out to our youth in the *"spirit of truth, awareness and understanding"* to make the *"Black Experience"* better for future generations.

"From Kingdom to nigger-dom" utilizes commentary, poetry, prose and candid introspection of the Black historical journey to remind us of how things were in times past and in some instances still are. I believe poetry to be the *"unbridled voice"* and *"imaginative key"*

of the changing times, which pierces the hearts and stirs the minds of each and every passing generation.

This publication serves to remind us of a commonly overlooked fact when it comes to living the *"Black Experience"*. So let us not forget that Black life with all of its challenges, nuances and intricacies has for itself the results of the experiential distance traveled, which often times is interpreted and expressed differently by those who have reached their destinations.

Some may view the distance traveled as a *"marvelous journey"*, wherein others might well view the distance traveled as only a *"trip"*. I believe Black life to be a *"collective journey defined by shared experiences"*, wherein the *"trip is defined by the destination sought"* and oftentimes the experiential distance is traveled alone.

You are personally invited to journey through the cultural twists, turns and nuances of the *"Collective Black Experience"* that is expressed in this most informative and provocative publication.

"From Kingdom to nigger-dom" provides a patented and historically candid introduction into the *"composite life experiences" of "Black People in North America"*. Ones who were racially branded and trade labelled *"niggers"* by white southerners residing in the British-American colonies. *You are encouraged to accept the experiential challenge of sharing the cultural journey!!!*

Buckle up, relax and enjoy the read!!!

Charles E. Dickerson

"Why Does It Always...

Have To Be About Color?"

This question was posed to me many years ago by one of our genetically evolved African sisters of the White persuasion… "A little bird tells me that you can never remember my name. Why is that? And another thing… why does it always have to be about color?"

An honest answer to this question is probably best understood based upon an experience that my young nephew and I shared several decades ago. I can remember the two of us entering their family's back yard, while engaging one another in general conversation and surprisingly the conversation abruptly ceased. My nephew who was only six years old at the time was silenced and stilled by a deeply entrenched scar located at the base of their gate. Now in his early 50s and a successful attorney in Atlanta, Georgia, he the small child persistently asked the question… "*Why is the earth scarred beneath the gate?"*

I can vividly remember being taken to task by this inquisitive and incredibly perceptive six year old, whose mind was bent on receiving a much deeper answer than I was prepared to give. I began by explaining how the weight and movement of the gate must have caused the scar to the earth beneath it, which appeared evident by the damage that was left behind in times past as the gate swung open and shut.

And he responded by asking... "Ok Unc, ok, but why is the earth scarred beneath the gate?" So I continued by telling him that the gate may have been mounted too close to the ground, causing it to scrape the surface of the earth beneath it, thereby causing the scar.

And again he asked... "Ok Unc, ok, but why is the earth scarred beneath the gate?" I continued to explain that the gate may have been mounted properly in the beginning, but over time the hinges of the gate may have been weakened due to repeated use, causing the gate to sag and scrape the surface of the earth beneath it, thereby causing the scar.

And again he responded by asking... "Ok Unc, ok, but why is the earth scarred beneath the gate?" I tried again by stating that the ground could have been uneven when the gate was installed, which could have caused the gate to scrape the surface of the earth beneath it, thereby causing the scar.

And again he responded by asking... "Ok Unc, ok, but why is the earth scarred beneath the gate?" So after growing somewhat irritated I stated that the possibility existed that the gate was not level in the first place.

And with even greater determination and inquisitiveness Cerille asked... "Ok Unc, just tell me... why is the earth scarred beneath the gate?" Having grown totally irritated with what appeared to be a cross examination by a young six year old kid, I stated the following in a rather commanding tone: *"Ok my little nephew, I was not here when the damage was done... so I don't have a precise answer. However, the scar remains as proof that damage did occur, and the damage serves as a reminder that the "question of why" needs to be asked, in order for the scar to speak and tell its own story."*

In retrospect, I should have known at that very moment that this brilliant, determined little kid would someday grow up to become an outstanding lawyer. So the moral of the story is this... the ground had most certainly experienced damage, which was evidenced by the compacted, marred, and scarred earth. It was also evident that the gate had left a visible scar that remained after a prolonged period of time. Even though the gate had since been adjusted and did not scrape the ground any longer, the imprint of the scar was an obvious reminder that repeated damage had been done in the past.

This isolated event brought to mind the *"floodgate of British colonial migration"* that opened wide to greet millions of European settlers upon their arrival into the Americas as free immigrants, only for them to flow freely into the *"municipal colonies"* of Jamestown and the twelve remaining colonies that followed. These thirteen colonies would later become the founding group of states from which the United States of America would be formed.

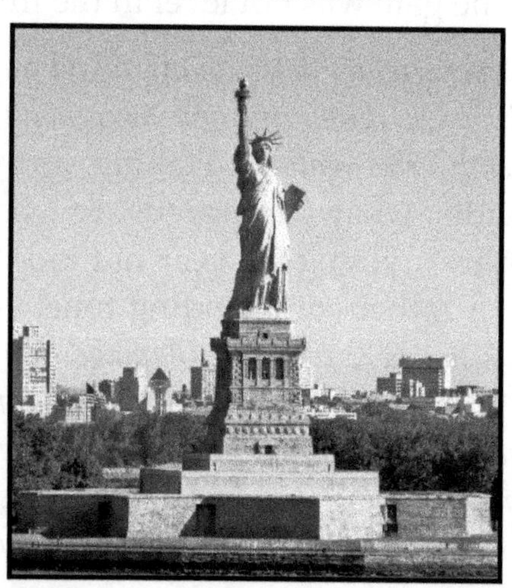

At the very same time the *"floodgate of British colonial forced-migration"* opened wide to receive 305,326 Africans into America out of the documented 12,521,336 that entered into the Americas by brutality and force. In fact the undocumented entries places these numbers tens of thousands and miliions higher.

These were in effect *"work colonies"* that had been established for the sole purpose of extracting free labor perpetually. Beginning in 1863, President Abraham Lincoln emancipated the Blacks that were enslaved in *"work colonies"* in 10 of the 13 states. In 1865 slavery was abolished in all the American states when the Union Army defeated the Confederacy.

These *"work colonies"*, although gone would later serve as *"templates of containment"* for the emancipated slaves. Once the plantation system was abolished, it morphed into a *"predominately Black penal colony network"*. The NAACP Criminal Justice Fact Sheet state that *"African Americans now constitute nearly 1 million of the total 2.3 million incarcerated population."*, although African Americans only make up 13.6% of the total U.S. population.

Today the *"penal colony network"* of old is known as the *"State and Federal Prison Systems"* that became famous for its *"work crews"* and *"chain gangs"* in the 1830s. The prison system in its earlier stages used prison labor in the form of *"institutionalized free labor"* to augment a wide variety of labor intensive tasks that were previously performed by slaves on the plantations.

The grave inequity and disparity between the two systems and societies, which were composed of the free European immigrants and the enslaved Africans whom were brought to America under the system of forced migration, would create the uneven foundation upon which the gate of freedom and prosperity rested. This would explain the cause of the permanently engraved scar that is etched in the hearts and minds of all people of color and their descendants whom entered the Americas by way of the Trans-Atlantic Slave Trade and not by way of Ellis Island. Only now do I realize and understand the gravity of the persistent question posed by my young nephew... "*Why is the earth scarred beneath the gate?*"

Even though the *"gate of forced migration"* has since been dismantled and does not scrape the constitutional foundation upon which America is firmly established, there is no disputing that the "GATE TO FREEDOM AND PROSPERITY" swung open for Europeans and swung close for Africans for several centuries and the *"indelible scar"* serves as a symbol of friction and resistance until this day. If on today one were to engage that very foundation upon which the *"gate of forced migration"* once rested for any appreciable amount of time as all Black Americans are compelled to do, it would be impossible to escape the uneven foundation upon which the *"gate of forced migration"* once stood that caused the *"indelible scar"*.

Regardless of how lightly one might tread upon that ground, once aggravated the very foundation upon which the *"gate of forced migration"* rested will began to break open the bonds of residual pain and solitary silence and the scar will begin to speak. The scar serves as a *"time-honored symbol unto itself"* and will in its own way speak to us... *be it out of humor, anger, social demonstration, or repudiation, it will speak!!!*

So when *"Black People"* who have passed through that gate make casual reference to something being a *"thing of blackness"*, we have earned the right for it to be about color, when the things about which we speak pertain to our unique experience of having been scarred by a system of slavery based solely upon race and color. So I am not surprised that many would question *"the scar"* as my young nephew once did, especially those who've reaped the benefits of the uneven foundation upon which the "GATE OF INEQUALITY AND SEPARATISM" once rested. It is only natural that one would question a Black person's reference to color when viewed from an elevated position of unbridled wealth and opportunity, while at the same time gazing down upon the *"scar of injustice and inequality"* while challenging the right of the scar to speak. The scar is a vocal reminder of the late Dr. Maya Angelou's 1969 critically acclaimed autobiography... *"I Know Why The Caged Bird Sings"!!!*

This long overdue body of work salutes the scar, for it has declared itself an instrument that is worthy to speak out from within the social abrasion and centuries of pain to those who look upon the scar and dare to question what it has to say. This book was written to speak to those who disregard the scar, while lacking empathy for its residual pain. *"From Kingdom to nigger-dom... A People Lost In Translation"* acknowledges that the *"ones who dare to question"* were not the "*irresponsible gatekeepers*", although they have been blessed by the discretionary openings and closings of the gate, present and in times past.

The gate about which this book speaks controlled the floodgate of *slavery, oppression, degradation, segregation, inequality, hatred and abuse* for Black People past and present. The uneven foundation upon which we tread has the historical right and moral obligation to speak freely concerning the *"indelible scar"* that reveals the residual pain of the gate that has become an integral part of the foundational story that opens wide to provide access to the *"American Dream"*.

It is important to note that you the 21st century offsprings of the European colonial immigrants are not held responsible as keepers of the gateway of *"free immigration"* and *"forged migration"* when the gate of injustice swung to and fro on the backwards hinges of racism! When it comes to the question of Black peculiarity and our uniquely patented response to "OUR UNIQUE EXPERIENCE", we consider ourselves justified in saying... *"It's a Black thing"*. But how silly of us to expect you *"a child of the gate"*, being culturally attached to the backwards and weakened hinges of the gate that has been silenced by time, opposition, and revolt to understand the *"indelible scar"* that only we the African Americas can relate to.

Of course there are those whom believe themselves to be unhinged and yet have the audacity to stand on the uneven foundation and place their ear to the scarred earth and ask... "*Why does it always have to be about color?*" I along with a multitude of others speak in the spirited voives of our ancestors and the spirit of God's love as we lift our heads and heavily laden hearts from the scarred earth and ask... *why not*? I offer you and others that may think and believe your question fitting, the following question... *"Why should a saga riddled with the irony of color not speak of color?"*

I truly believe that God in His majesty and wisdom blesses the scarred earth to speak. It is from the Lord's prophetic teachings that we shall all come to know that even the bad is nourishment for the good when it pleases the Lord to heal the land as it is recorded in Proverbs chapter 22, verses 20 thru 23 {ESV}...

> *"Have I not written for you thirty sayings of counsel and knowledge, to make you know what is right and true, that you may give a true answer to those who sent you?*
>
> *Do not rob the poor, because he is poor, or crush the afflicted at the gate, for the LORD will plead their cause and rob of life those who rob them."*

I trust this response will be received in the spirit in which it is given, for it was not I that asked the question... "*Why does it always have to be about color?*"

~ The "n"-Word Explained ~

Continuation of a misguided saga!!!

There are many who ask... *"Why have a discussion about the "n"-Word"?* Undoubtedly there is a lot of ambivalence and twisted emotions associated with the word *"nigger"* and rightfully so. Yet, a large number of people continue to breathe life into it even until this day. While others attempt to close their ears, while hoping that it will be buried alive or simply go away.

NAACP delegates 'bury' N-word in ceremony

'We're taking it out of our spirit,' Detroit mayor says of racial slur

Yet, upon considering the magnitude of the social implications surrounding this extremely toxic and most incendiary word, I feel duty bound as a Black person, whom at the age of eight was subjected to and witnessed my mother being offended by its use, when I was called *"nigger"* by two middle aged adult Caucasian females, simply because I was Black.

This traumatic experience combined with the *"brewing controversy"* surrounding the continual use of the word provided the impetus needed to exhume and examine the *"alleged corpse"* at its source, which is absolutely essential to understanding its *origin, nature and prolonged life-cycle.* Unraveling the anguish, bitterness and pain that explains the social implications of the continued use of the word for nearly 400 years in the aftermath of its *"illegitimate birth"* has become a priority and a personal quest.

The *"n"-Word* as we have come to know it, has taken upon itself a stubborn resistance to social intolerance. The word has begun to live and thrive outside of the initial boundaries and social context in which it was initially prescribed.

Nigger... A Generic Trade Label or racial epitaph!!!

From its source, the word *"Niger"* served as a *"generic trade label"* springing forth from the Niger region of West Africa prior to derogatorily morphing into the word *"nigger"*. Wherein this simple little word matured and spread like a *"pandemic social disease"* that has continued to grow and function like a *"cancer"* without a cure.

Like all things that have life, the life that is perpetuated in the word *"nigger"* is manifested out of an arduous process of pain and inescapable *degradation and subjugation without deliverance* for the majority of Black People. Since its birth, the word *"nigger"* has withstood every test of endurance and attempted annihilation, only to continue to live and resonate in the hearts and minds of those whom relish it's sorted and twisted existence with little concern for its terribly painful and misguided past.

The word "nigger" survives wars and rebellions!!!

Who would have imagined that the use of the word *"nigger"* would have survived the Trans-Atlantic Slave Trade, British Colonialism, Indian Wars, Shay's Rebellion, Whiskey Rebellion, Fries' Rebellion, Barbary Wars, War of 1812, Mexican-American War, U.S. Slave Rebellions, Bleeding Kansas, Brown's Raid on Harper's Ferry, American slavery, American Civil War, Emancipation, American Reconstruction, Spanish-American War, U.S.-Philippine War, Boxer Rebellion, World War I, Great Depression, World War II, the Cold War, Korean War, Vietnam War, Iranian Hostage Crisis, U.S. Libya

Conflict, U.S. Invasion of Grenada, U.S. Invasion of Panama, Persian Gulf War *("Operation Desert Storm")*, World Trade Center and Pentagon attacks by Osama bin Laden & Al Qaeda, Afghanistan War *("Operation Enduring Freedom")*, and Persian Gulf War *("Operation Iraqi Freedom")* among other minor military conflicts, wherein Black People sacrificed, struggled, fought, and died for America's continued independence.

Nigger... Memorialized and buried, yet it lives!!!

One decade ago the NAACP took on the mission of burying the so-called *"n"-Word*, only to find that the word continues to thrive and survive on *"life support"*. Ironically, its lingering survival is supported by Blacks who complain of being offended by its use by the descendants of those whom conceived and fostered it.

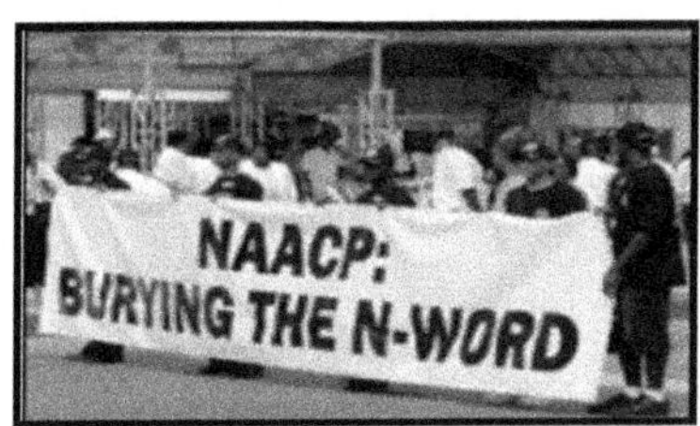

In fact the *"n"-Word* was buried in seriousness by the NAACP, but its symbolism was received in jest by a number of Black People. For if it had been a human corpse the burial would have been ruled an act of *"attempted murder"* and treated as a capital crime, simply because the word *"nigger"* was buried alive.

The word *"nigger"* has been condemned to *"death by lethal rejection"* in the public arena, due to the social pressures applied to the descendants of those whom fostered the word in the first place. Yet, the robust life that is continually witnessed is being breathed back into it by Black People who have become *"socially conditioned enigmatic human respirators"*. Sadly enough, far too many 21st century Black Folk are guilty of enabling its continued existence and use for reasons that defy human logic and rational comprehension.

Based upon the ceremony and pomp surrounding its burial and the nationwide news coverage that was provided by CBS, CNN, NBC, BBC, Washington Post, Associated Press, The New York Times, USA Today, and The Detroit News among others, one would have thought the *"n"-Word* was in fact dead and permanently buried, only for it to continue to rear its ugly head and profanely speak on an ongoing basis.

I believe Reverend Otis Moss III, the Assistant Pastor of Trinity United Church of Christ located in Chicago, Illinois said it best when eulogizing the *"n"-Word* on July 9, 2007 upon stating the following concerning the word *"nigger"*...

"This was the greatest child that racism ever birthed..."

"The "n"-Word Gone Forever"

...or is it???

The new teachers of cultural dis-enlightenment!!!

This work has been written for everyone that is familiar with the 14th letter of the English alphabet, realizing that not everyone that read it will receive the message and agree.

The *"unsavory truth"* is that any unwelcomed pattern of social behavior will not be completely extinguished until the teachers of such behavior die out. When the *"enlightened ones"* among us abandon its use, in due time the *"socially unacceptable use"* of the word *"nigger"* will eventually go away, thereby sanctioning its *"official death"* and *"proper burial"*.

The *"teachers"* in this particular case includes both Whites and Blacks alike, who profane the letter *"n"* by continuing to use the word *"nigger"* and its *"derivatives"*, which has been reintroduced into the American society and it's lexicon as the *"n"-Word.*

Cultural and social implications of the word nigger!!!

For one to understand and fully appreciate the importance of discontinuing the use of the word *"nigger"*, we have to revisit the use of the word in its initial historical context to fully comprehend its *"social significance"* in the minds of White People, relative to the *"cultural dilemma"* that it poses for millions of America's African slave descendants.

When it comes to understanding this problem and addressing it at its root, I believe Malcolm X said it best in his speech, *"Message to the Grassroots"* that he gave at the Northern Negro Grass Roots Leadership Conference on November 10, 1963 *(Available, Youtube)*. The conference was held at the King Solomon Baptist Church in Detroit, Michigan just fourteen weeks prior to Malcolm's brutal assassination, which occurred following his split from the Nation of Islam.

Malcolm had this to say regarding the study of history...

"Of all our studies, history is best qualified to reward our research".

The study of West African history and its role in the Trans-Atlantic Slave Trade *(relative to the study of African American history)* is the key to understanding the fundamental problems of Black People in America, whom were forced into slavery to be used as the "ECONOMIC ENGINE" for constructing the *"New World"*.

When African Americans dig deep enough into the history of West Africa as it pertains to the history of British colonial slavery in America, we will find *"nigger" and "property"* buried at the root of our *social, political, economic and family problems*.

- *Social* - Integration opened the door to social access for Blacks leading to the development of *"prejudice premium zones"* commonly known as *"suburbia"*. HUD *(Department of Housing and Urban Development)* was established in the aftermath of the Civil Rights Movement for the purpose of overseeing and managing the deployment of Blacks into previously owned and occupied White communities. PUD *(Planned Urban Development)* and recently enacted *"Stand Your Ground Laws"* are designed to work in unison for the purpose of redeploying Whites back into the urban centers that were abandoned by their predecessors beginning in the 1960s, when *"white flight"* took the form of a diaspora with inner city Whites flooding into the suburbs to escape and buffer themselves from the presence of Black People.
- *Political* - The birth of the Electoral College grew out of the pro-slavery movement as a means of buffering the vote in plantation districts and low White population areas with large concentrations of slaves *(without citizenship)* that were counted as 3/5 of a person in voter representation.

  The Electoral College came about as a result of the *"Three-Fifths Compromise" (Article 1, Section*

2, *Paragraph 3 - US Constitution)*. The disparity was rectified by mandating 2 senators per state regardless of the state's population, leading to the disparity between the electoral votes outweighing the popular vote, which always leans conservative in national / presidential elections *(Al Gore vs. George W. Bush in the year 2000 and Hilary Clinton vs. Donald Trump in the year 2016)*.

Voting rights and gerrymandering in addition to criminalization of the Black Race are measures that are designed to reduce the voting role of Blacks by miscellaneous means and felony convictions that are designed to favor whites as lessor offenders over Blacks.

- Economic - Unfair hiring practices, wage disparity, basic imbalance of economic empowerment, and historic job discrimination favoring Whites over Blacks.
- Family – The *"Willie Lynch Letter : The Making of a Slave"* is "THE BLUEPRINT" that was deployed during slavery for future containment, division, status reduction, and the ongoing plan to eliminate the Black male from the Black family equation. This racist agenda was further compounded by the welfare system guidelines of banning non-related Black males from household receiving aid, promoting the one parent Black family structure that is rapidly becoming the *"new Black family model"* of today.

Most importantly we need to understand that all of the anti-social measures and means that are used to target Black males, especially the younger Black males are systematically done for the purpose of *"population and voter control"*. The predatory police killings, high levels of incarceration, and role reversal between the male and female in the Black family are in the *the "Willie Lynch Letter"*. These measures were designed to quarantine the fertile Black and White females from the Black males' sperm.

All of these measures work in unison as *"birth control measures"* by isolating and destroying Black sperm donors for the purpose of suppressing child birth in favor of the Whites. *{Read - Willie Lynch Letter}*

The word nigger revisited at its source!!!

The saga of Africa's modern day American descendants began as an unbelievable tale of nightmarish proportion that redefined the *treatment boundaries* and *subject identity* of captives whom were initially kidnapped and forced-purchased into slavery for the purpose of constructing the *"New World"*.

In times past, prior to the Trans-Atlantic Slave Trade, slavery was based solely upon the loss of one's freedom, wherein the enslaved individuals became the servant property of another. In fact, slavery is not new; slavery has existed in various nations and lands since the dawn of humanity and the advent of mankind. Slavery is defined as...

> a. *"the state of a person who is a chattel of another"*
>
> b. *"something (such as a slave, piece of furniture, tool, etc.) that a person owns other than land or buildings."*

African slavery and its people!!!

African slavery existed long before there was an America and did not have its beginning with the Trans-Atlantic Slave Trade. Slavery in the Americas sprang from the birth of European enslavement that was forced upon Africans that had its beginning in the year 1441 A.D. with the Portuguese, whom initiated the practice of forcefully capturing Africans and trading them to the Europeans. Slavery in the Americas was considerably different from earlier forms of slavery dating back to the ancient civilizations of the Samaritans, Egyptians, Byzantines, and the Ottomans, among others. The earliest official record of slavery can be traced back to 1760 B.C. in Samaria, wherein the following is recorded in the Code of Hammurabi: *{Example: Law #15}*

> *"If anyone take a male or female slave of the court, or a male or female slave of a freedman, outside the city gates, he shall be put to death."*

Those who lost their freedom to slavery prior to the Trans-Atlantic Slave Trade were fortunate considering they were allowed to retain their *cultural identities.* Unlike British colonial slavery in America, wherein the slaves were stripped of their *generational, historical, social, religious, ethnic, and personal identities,* which in effect constitutes *"institutionally prescribed nigger-dom"*? *In fact, "terrorism" and "identity theft" are believed to be a recent phenomenon, but both had their beginnings with the "life-lock" of British colonial slavery!!!*

For this cause, Black People have a vested interest in learning the true knowledge of their cultural past that existed long before British colonial slavery began.

It is vitally important for Black People to understand that our historic beginning did not start with the off-loading of African captives from the slave ships that brought our ancestors to the American shores. For many of us, we treat our inception into the American experience as if our African ancestors signed up and agreed to a seven day Trans-Atlantic Cruise to America, only for the *"mythical cruise liners"* to breakdown at the scheduled time of departure, wherein our forefathers thought it best to remain in America and voluntarily work forever for free.

Well the truth of the matter is our West African ancestors did not arrive here in glee, sipping martinis, and drinking cocktails. Of course many would choose to simply close their minds to the truth, while immersing themselves in self-induced amnesia.

Malcolm X... *"we didn't land on Plymouth Rock,*

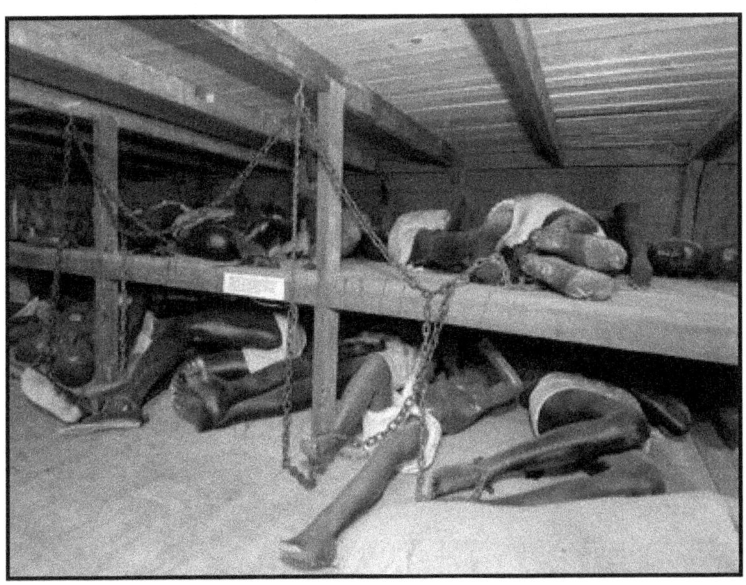

Plymouth Rock landed on us".

In fact the Mayflower and its host fleet of seafaring vessels were the 17th, 18th, and 19th century trans-Atlantic European cruise liners for the European immigrants who passed thru Ellis Island to become colonial settlers and American citizens, but not us.

The "Middle Passage" and its "floating hell holes"!!!

The story of Africans forced migration into the Americas was far different for the African captives whom found themselves strapped down and stored like sardines in the stench filled cargo holes of the slave transport vessels that journeyed to and fro across the Atlantic Ocean for 246 years, bringing Africa's precious human cargo to the Americas without a return option.

Unfortunately for the tens of millions that did survive the journey the transport vessels were nothing more than floating time capsules and *"life-long retarding incubators"* for those that survived the narrow storage confines of the lower deck compartments of those dreaded seafaring vessels.

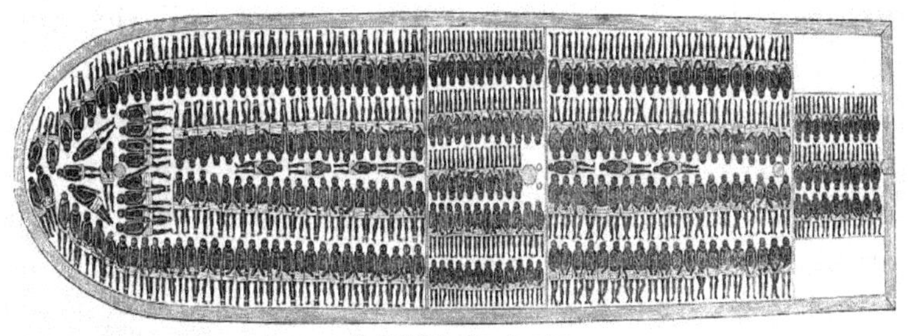
(Vue de la batterie basse d'un navire negrier.)

~ Slave Ship Granger ~

The original slave transport ships and the countless fleets of *"floating hell holes"* that traversed the treacherous Atlantic Ocean were death traps for countless millions of non-surviving African captives.

When we make the conscious choice of tracing our beginning back to the docking ramps of the various coastal shipping ports of colonial America and ending our search there, we not only do ourselves a grave disservice, but we also cripple those that come after us.

A once glorious people lost in translation!!!

As a matter of future preparation, African Americans need to know that our native African forefathers came from a glorious past, prior to the European conquest of African enslavement. This knowledge would rid Blacks of the *"low ethnic esteem"* that negatively impacts us as a group. Esteem is the *"estimated outpouring"* originating from its root word *"teem"*, which means to *"pour out"*. It is impossible to estimate what and how much can be poured out of you, if you have no knowledge of what and how much has been poured into you by your ancestors.

When we allow ourselves and others to trace our

historical beginning back to the auction galleries and plantations and end our search there, we position ourselves to be defined as ***"a non-distinct race of people lost in translation"***. The psychic tendency is to view ourselves as the *beggar* that got off the slave ship versus the *banker* that got on, or the *thief* that got off versus the *priest* that got on, or the *prostitute* that got off versus the *queen* that got on. We have been conditioned to accept the oppressors curse and disregard our blessing of heritage and prior greatness.

~ Charleston, SC Slave Market ~

The ancestral knowledge of Black People is essential to erasing the awful stigma that has been ascribed to us by our European slave masters of yesterday and only we can change the prevailing narrative and negative perception of ourselves. Our failure to reconnect with our history and greatness resigns us to the fate of a downtrodden people.

West Africans... Targets of European possession!!!

Our African and mulatto forefathers were labeled *"niggers"* in accordance with the commercial trade practices of the 16th through the 19th centuries that identified and labeled African captives based upon the regional areas from whence they were taken.

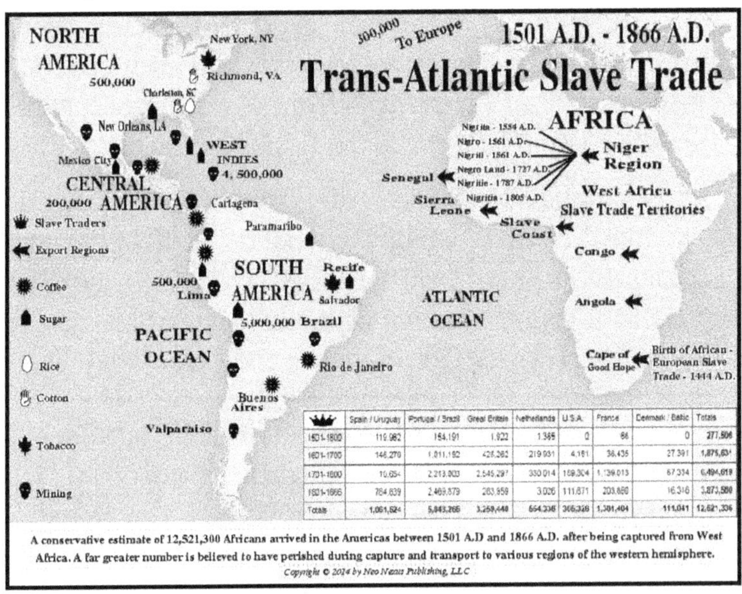

	Spain / Uruguay	Portugal / Brazil	Great Britain	Netherlands	U.S.A.	France	Denmark / Baltic	Totals
1501-1600	119,982	154,191	1,922	1,365	0	66	0	277,506
1601-1700	146,270	1,011,192	428,262	219,931	4,181	36,435	27,391	1,875,631
1701-1800	10,654	2,213,003	2,545,297	330,014	189,304	1,139,013	67,334	6,494,619
1801-1866	784,639	2,469,879	283,959	3,026	111,871	203,850	16,316	3,873,580
Totals	1,061,524	5,843,265	3,259,440	554,336	305,326	1,381,404	111,041	12,521,336

A conservative estimate of 12,521,300 Africans arrived in the Americas between 1501 A.D and 1866 A.D. after being captured from West Africa. A far greater number is believed to have perished during capture and transport to various regions of the western hemisphere.

Cartography, which is the study and practice of mapmaking indicates that European maps from the late 19th and early 20th century were characterized by efforts on behalf of the colonial powers to identify the geographical areas from which their future possessions would be acquired.

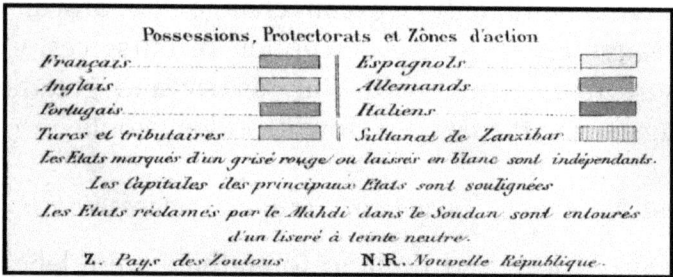

Gravé et Imp. par Erhard _ 2e tirage, 1888

Possessions, Protectorats et Zônes d'action

Français		Espagnols	
Anglais		Allemands	
Portugais		Italiens	
Turcs et tributaires		Sultanat de Zanzibar	

Les Etats marqués d'un grisé rouge ou laissés en blanc sont indépendants.

Les Capitales des principaux Etats sont soulignées

Les Etats réclamés par le Mahdi dans le Soudan sont entourés d'un liseré à teinte neutre.

Z. Pays des Zoulous   N.R. Nouvelle République

European maps of 19th and 20th century Africa identified areas abundant in raw material, mercantile goods and other targeted exports. European colonial maps of West Africa from the 16th through the mid-19th century were different, in that humans were identified as *"targets of possession"*. Slaves were *"the new commodity of extraction"* from the Niger Region, when the *"Trans-Atlantic Slave Trade"* began.

Early maps of Africa identify *"Niger"* as the derivative source from whence all of the *"EUROPEAN_GENERIC TRADE LABELS"* were derived that served to identify *"human captives"*, regardless of the areas and territories from whence they were taken.

An examination of the territorial labels that are inscribed on European colonial maps of West Africa, beginning in the 16th through the 19th century is the "critical key" to identifying the origin and misapplication of the word "nigger".

Maps speak volumes about the present and the past. As early as 1554 A.D. foreign maps of Africa were being imprinted with the inscriptions *"Nigrita"*, *"Nigro"*, *Nigriti*, *"Negro Land"*, *"Nigritie"*, *and*

"Nigritia" identifying geographical defined areas of colonial slave acquisition within the Niger Region.

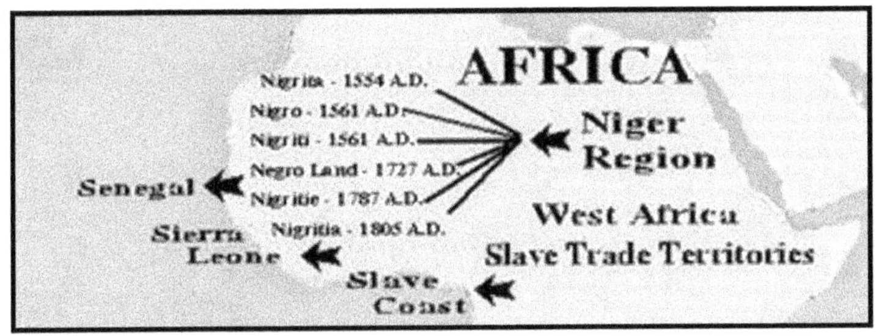

The territorial labels applied to the maps were inspired by their European colonizers. The natives were initially *kidnapped, stolen, and forced-purchased* before being traded and auctioned off in a loosely, coercive, mutual arrangement as *"niggers"*. *In essence, the colonial maps represent the "X" that marks the spot!!!*

Niger region... Targeted areas of slave acquisition!!!

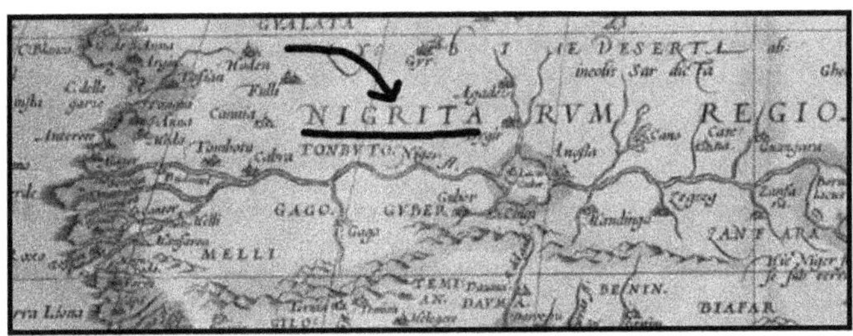

1554 (Nigrita)

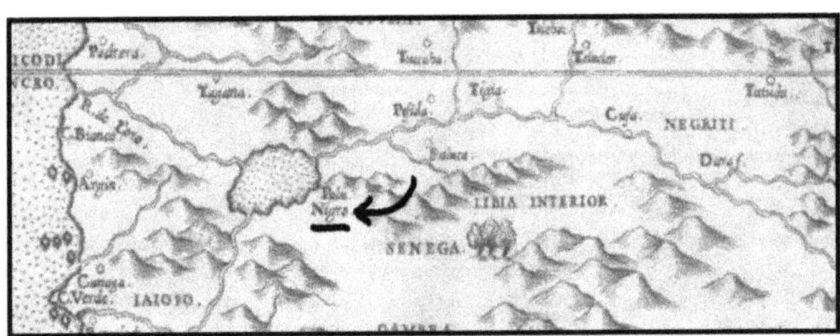

1561 (Nigro)

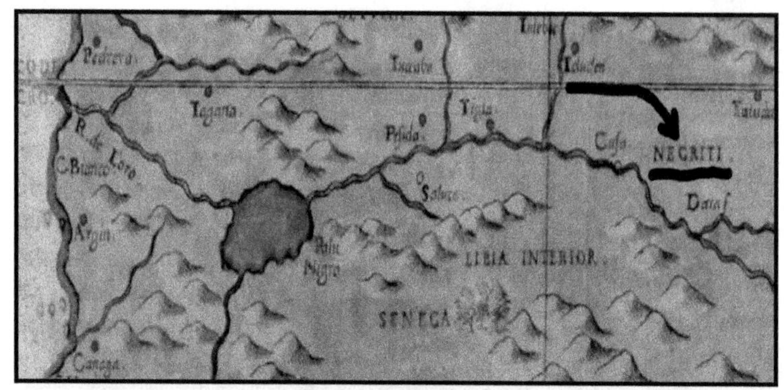

1575 (Nigriti)

1727 (Negro Land)

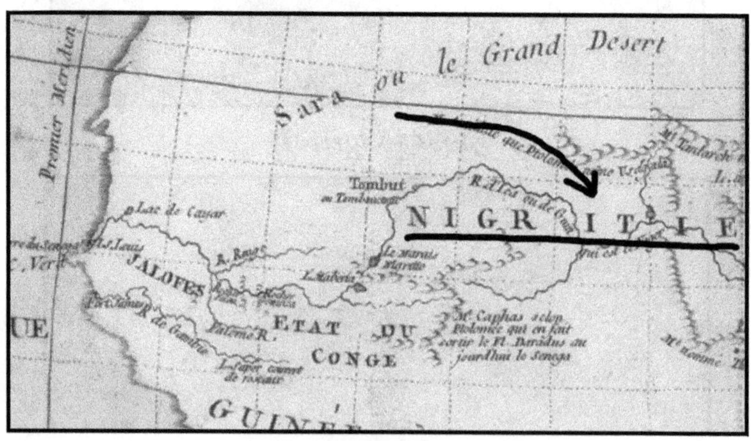

1787 (Nigritie)

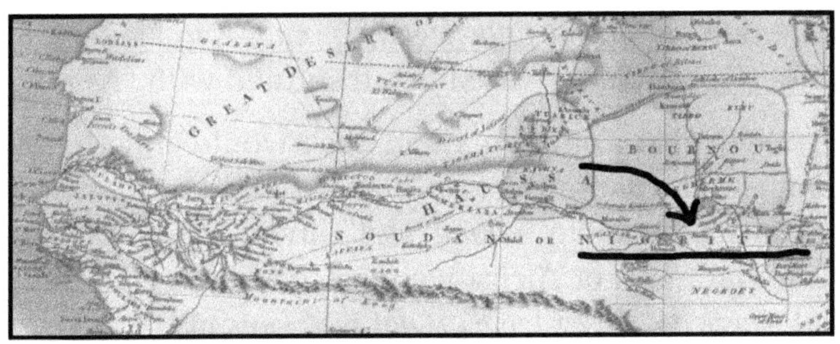

1805 (Nigritia)

How the word "nigger" came to be!!!

The word *"nigger"* evolved from the word *"Niger"*. *"Niger"* originated as a neutral term referring to people with black skin, a variation of the Spanish and Portuguese noun Negro, descendant from the Latin adjective niger *("black")*. In the 1520s Leo Africanus, a Moorish diplomat and author identified the *"region of Niger"* when referring to Africa's 3rd largest river as the *"river Niger"* located in the land of the Blacks.

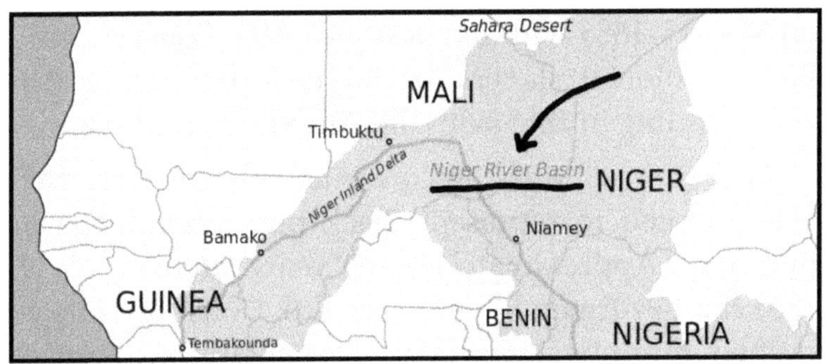

The word *"nigger"* is a *"descriptive thorn of rejection"* that was used to relegate the enslaved Africans to a *"last-class status"*. Prior to and after abolition it was common practice for Blacks to be referred to as *"nigger boy"* and *"nigger girl"* designating them as *"property"*. *"Nigger"* was rendered *"obsolete" by*

abolition *causing it to be legally annulled on the basis of property*, wherein it was later substituted with *"Negro"*.

Negro is a common noun that would inherit the English word usage of a *"proper noun"*, making it a socially acceptable *"ethnic label"* under the law. Early Colonial maps of Africa were inscribed *"Negro Land"*, *but where is "nigger land", if not the "Land of Dixie"?*

The word *"nigger"* did not begin as a *"racial slur"*, although it did evolve into a *"derogatory badge of rejection"* due to slavery, later functioning to ridicule and exclude, in addition to relegating the African captives to centuries of inhumane bondage, coupled with *physical, psychological, verbal,* and *sexual abuses.*

Trans-Atlantic Slave Trade and its vestiges!!!

The Portuguese originated the Trans-Atlantic Slave Trade in 1444 with the capture of 235 Africans in 1441. The practice lasted 444 years before ending in Brazil on May 13, 1888 with the passage of the *"Golden Law"*. British colonial slavery began in 1619, lasting 246 years, ending in 1865 with the American Civil War.

At the outset of the Reconstruction Period *"Negro"* was adopted to represent Black personhood, but in title only. Approximately three years later on July 9, 1868 the 14th Amendment to the U.S. Constitution was ratified granting citizenship *"to 'all persons born or naturalized in the United States,' which included former slaves recently freed."* The 14th Amendment elevated Negroes to the status of *"fully vested human beings"*, no longer legally deemed *"three-fifths of a person"*.

Though constitutionally free, Blacks were still

treated as *"second-class citizens"* under Jim Crow Laws, which were complimented with a constitutional loophole in the 13th Amendment allowing for its continuance for *"convicted criminals"*.

> **Section 1.** *Neither slavery nor involuntary servitude,* ***except as a punishment for crime whereof the party shall have been duly convicted****, shall exist within the United States, or any place subject to their jurisdiction.*
>
> **Section 2.** *Congress shall have power to enforce this article by appropriate legislation.*

This *"constitutionally sacred allowance"* paved the way for America's *"first prison bill"* that was passed by congress. Section one of the 13th Amendment left the door opened for a *"backdoor form of slavery"* that was immediately exploited to rebuild the southern economy and its infrastructure in the aftermath of the civil war. Shortly after its passage flagrant arrests were made from among the 4,000,000 unemployed previously freed black slaves, whom for the most part had no safe place to go and were consider *"vagrant de facto citizens"* needing to be arrested and put to work on behalf of the southern states and their constituents.

Criminalization of the Black race became the underlying theme of local and national politics, social policy, and race relations in American society leading up to the present, wherein 30% of the Black male population in Alabama have lost their right to vote.

The Bureau of Justice reported that 1 in 3 young Black males are expected to go to jail or prison in their lifetime. Black men account for 6.5% of the American population and make up 40.2% of the prison population. Upon being convicted of a felony offence,

Blacks are automatically reduced to *"3/5 of a person"* all over again, lacking fully vested citizenry rights.

Mass incarceration is the new form of Jim Crow that has morphed out of the evolutionary measures of racial containment born out Section 1 of the 13th Amendment to the U.S. Constitution. Jim Crow Laws were *"racial segregation laws"* enacted between 1870 and 1959 for the purpose of *economic restrictions, social containment, and political immobilization (*See Timeline – Ferris State University (FSU), Jim Crow Museum).*

I find it interesting that a current map of West Africa can be visited and upon viewing the coastal interior we will come upon two countries that are literally screaming out to us *"in name"*, revealing the source from whence the word *"nigger"* was derived. Those countries are... *Niger and Nigeria. Niger is a Latin word meaning "black"; pronounced Negro in Spanish and Portuguese. Nigeria is an extension of Niger, and "nigger" is believed to be a mispronunciation of Niger by Southern Whites, when used as an "identifier of common origin" for our West African ancestors, whom were brought here as chattel property by their European traders.*

The following is quoted from the African American Registry, courtesy of Dr. David Pilgrim (FSU):

> *"In early modern French, niger became negre and, later, negress (Black woman) was unmistakably a part of language history.*
>
> *One can compare to negre the derogatory nigger and earlier English substitutes such as negar, neegar, neger, and niggor that developed into its lexico-semantic true version in English.*

It is probable that nigger is a phonetic spelling of the White Southern mispronunciation of Negro."

As a matter of fact, the word *"nigger"* was rendered obsolete in the aftermath of the American Civil War when the *Confederate Government, its currency and slave-based economy* ceased to exist; similar to the *"Confederate Flag"* that symbolized the *"INSTITUTION OF SLAVERY"* and the *"Confederate Money"* that it once generated.

THE "CONFEDERATE 'WAR' FLAG",

"CONFEDERATE MONEY"

& "NIGGER" IS OBSOLETE!!!

Origin and evolution of the word "nigger"!!!

Upon researching the origin and evolution of the word *"nigger"*, it is not surprising to find that it has been relegated to the *"taboo column"* in American society in the form of the *"n"-Word"*, which in itself is nothing more than a *"derogatorily ostracized pseudonym"*.

> ***Pseudonym...*** *"a name that a person or group assumes for a particular purpose, which can differ from his or her original or true name."*

A personal review of language history reveals an interesting fact, wherein only one word other than *"nigger or niggers"* which was derived from the true name of the slaves place of origin *"Niger or Nigers"* has undergone a phonetic transformation from acceptable word usage in the language of a people to a *"self-imposed pseudonym"*. This happened when the Hebrew word for *"GOD"* was relegated to the pseudonym "YHWH" *(pronounced "Yahweh" – "the 'Inexpressible Name' or 'Unutterable Name' of the God of Israel")*.

This was done by the Levitical Priesthood during the Old Testament era. In this particular instance, the word for *"GOD"*, namely *"Yahweh"* *("THE MOST HIGH")*, the SELF-PROCLAIMED *"I AM THAT I AM"* was expressed as the pseudonym *"YHWH"* for strictly pious and puritanical reasons.

Now the word *"nigger"*, unlike the word *"GOD"*, *which represents the HIGHEST OF THE HIGH,* represents the *"lowest of the low"*. Thus causing it to be exiled into the *"bad word hall of fame"* in North American society, where it has been assigned the *"n-word"* pseudonym for strictly socially pandemic reasons that serves as a euphemism to soften the impact of the word "nigger".

> ***Euphemism...*** *"the substitution of an agreeable or inoffensive expression for one that may offend or suggest something unpleasant."*

In review, it is plain to see how the word *"nigger"* having originated from *"Niger"*, conveys different images and meanings to different groups of people. Without knowledge of its origin, the sheer speaking of the word signifies different messages depending upon the *race, disposition, and social context* of the person or persons using it, be they White or Black. This denotes an evolution in the application of the word over an appreciable span of time during British colonial history and American history up until now.

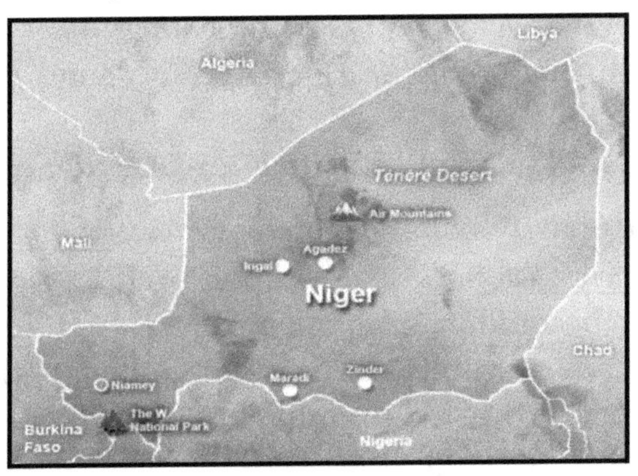

Initially the word *"Niger"* functioned as a *"generic trade label"* that was affixed to all African captives brought into the North American British colonies, prior to being sold at auction and assigned *"proper names"*. Beginning in 1514 A.D. the African captives were being shipped from Sierra Leone and other coastal outposts into the various ports of entry in the New World. The *"generic trade label"* served as the captives' *"interim identifier"*, prior to them being placed on plantations wherein a *"first name"* was assigned by their owners that would become their property name.

The fact remains that the acquired subjects were traded and sold as *"captives without names"* to the

European merchants upon being taken from the European labelled West African areas of Nigrita, Nigro, Nigriti, Negro Land, Nigritie, and Nigritia. Between the points of acquisition and the points of sale the *British slave financiers, slave catchers, slave purchasers, slave transporters, slave merchants* referred to them as "*NIGERS*" in place of *Nigritas, Nigritis, Nigrities, Nigritias, Nigroes, or Negroes,* based upon the area in which they were taken. "*NIGER*" was used as an "*interim identifier*" to label the captives prior to the "*southern slave auctioneers*" and "*southern slave owners*" mispronunciation of "*NIGER*", which became "*nigger*".

Nigger...An "Interim Identifier" or "Racial Slur"?

Unfortunately, what began as an "*interim identifier*" for "*nameless captives*" based upon origin, prior to the captives becoming "*plantation slaves*" and receiving proper names, would ultimately become a permanent derogatory fixture of humiliation and verbal abuse.

In effect, the African captives were traded in bulk and sold without names by their African traders and European merchants. They remained *nameless* throughout the acquisition-to-auction process, at which time they were legally deemed slaves. They were later *dehumanized, prepped,* and *readied* for an extremely difficult and sometimes short, but extremely long utilitarian life on the "*plantation*". During the entire period of time they were being referred to as "*niggers*" by their handlers, while awaiting "*individual property names*".

Once on the plantations in the British colonies of America, the slaves received "*British property names*" *on a first name basis "only"*. A first name with no ties to family or cultural origin had the desired effect as do an *"inmate number"* that is assigned to convicts in the United States' Federal and State Penitentiary Systems today. *Inmate # "22843" was used to identify Malcolm X!*

Malcolm Little a/k/a Malcolm X was imprisoned from 1946 thru 1952. For 6 years Inmate Number "22843" identified Malcolm Little as Massachusetts' State Property.

El-Hajj Malik El-Shabazz {1925-1965}

Nigger...From private property to state property!!!

On and off of the plantations *"nigger"* was equivalent to *"convict"*, corresponding to "PROPERTY" and it carried the same social stigma and branding effect as it does today. The major difference is... unlike slaves on the plantations, the majority of today's prisoners are not confined forever and given good behavior they are allowed to go home. Slavery was different, there was no period of release and more importantly they had no home to return to. *The America continent was a "colonial Alcatraz" for the slaves!*

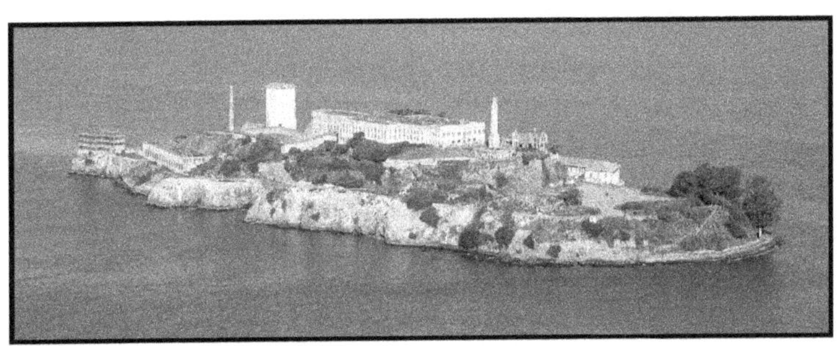

"Alcatraz Federal Penitentiary"

The North American continent, is virtually surrounded by water, making it very similar to the island of Alcatraz for the African slaves. Once on, it was virtually impossible to get off if you were a slave.

The surrounding waters served as a *"natural moat of captivity"* in both instances. America was the Confederate Alcatraz for Blacks before the Civil War!!!

Prison culture supplants early Hip Hop culture!!!

Unfortunately for African Americans, many young and middle aged male Blacks are *"emulating certain facets of prison behavior"*. By embracing *"sagging"* they are *"affirming the actions"* of those whom prefer that things return to the *"days of old"*. Sagging is a *"socially undesirable fashion of dress"* born out of prison culture.

Sagging is unmistakably a prison style of dress that congers up a mental image of Black People as *"post-dated niggers in the legal sense"*, attired in shabby dress. Sagging is an *"undesirable fashion statement"* that creates images of Black People as *"property of White People"* in the minds of those who relish the idea of all Black People as *"slave property"*, belonging in *"institutions"*. Prisons are extensions of the 16th through the 19th century plantations that were based on*"maximum containment"* and *"denial of citizenship"*.

"Sagging" and its *"distasteful bedfellows"* serve as an open invitation to the wantonly guilty parties to reenact the *"racial ills of the past"* that are reemerging out of a brutal and dehumanizing, historical context. This in-part could account for the increasing number of Blacks being killed by White policeman, relative to the loss of *"public sentiment"* by White Americans. ***Sagging is equivalent to wearing "red" in a bullfight!!!***

"Unfavorable Presentation"

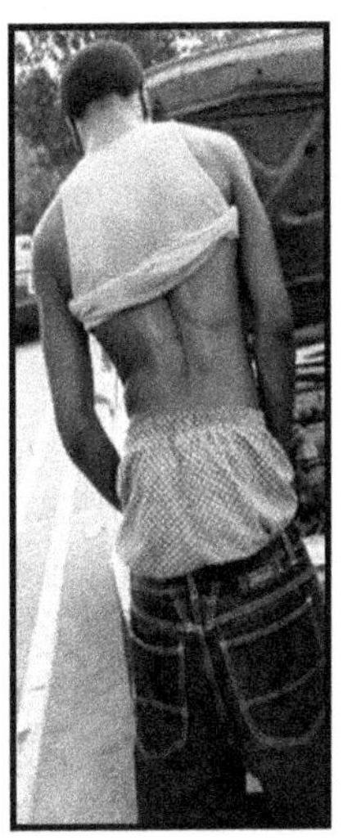

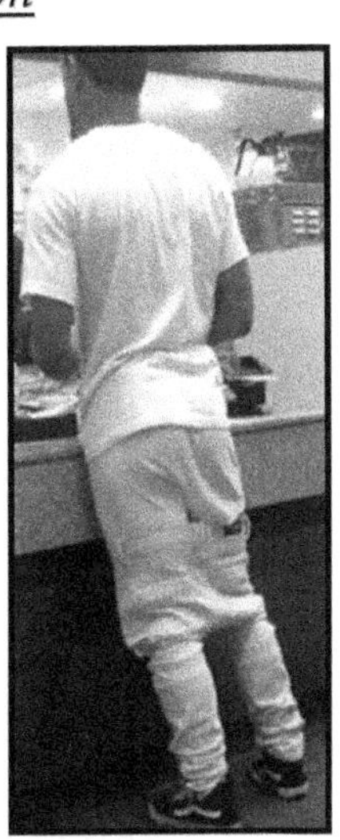

"Generates "negative invitation!!!"

Loss of public sentiment... Key to social injustice!!!

"Public sentiment" is the fundamental key to *"justice"* and *"consensus"* in a free society. In the absence of public sentiment very little can be accomplished.

> *"Sentiment"* is defined as... *"an attitude, thought, or judgment, prompted by feelings of love, sympathy, kindness, etc."*

"Public sentiment" is a social currency that translates into *"social acceptability"* without prejudice or unfair penalty, when embraced by the general public.

"Public sentiment" is measured by the opinions and attitudes of the general public in matters of social and legal concerns, requiring *"fairness in judgement"* for the achievement of *peace, justice, and equality.*

Republican senatorial candidate Abraham Lincoln made the following statement, while debating incumbent democratic Senator Stephen A. Douglas during the 1858 Lincoln-Douglas Debates. A series of seven debates took place that is historically referred to as *"The Great Debates of 1858"*.

"*In this and like communities, public sentiment is everything. With public sentiment, nothing can fail; without it, nothing can succeed."*

"Public sentiment" was the deciding factor that lay at the very heart of the *"anti-slavery"* versus *"pro-slavery"* debates that propelled Attorney Abraham Lincoln to senatorial victory, leading up to his 1860 Presidential election. *Public sentiment* played a major role in the abolition of slavery and the American Civil War, including the 13th, 14th, and 15th Amendments to the Constitution, wherein Negroes received citizenship, civil rights, and voting rights.

Now, some 150 years later Black People in America find themselves caught up in a similar battle involving *"the loss of public sentiment"*. The increasing numbers of Blacks being killed by *predatory White police officers* mirror the public lynchings that began during the Reconstruction Era, when *"public sentiment"* for Negroes was at its lowest at any time in America's post-slavery history.

Police Black Practice Targets... Police Black Shootings...

Police Black Killings... Black Lives Matter!!!

"Casual Killing Act" once dead... Now resurrected!!!

Without doubt, the ongoing rash of police killings of Black people that is being witnessed is the reinstitution of the *"Casual Killing Act"* that was enacted in the State of Virginia in October 1669, when *"public sentiment"* was at its very worst. The *"Casual Killing Act"* of 1669 and the predatory police killings of 21st century Blacks have one thing in common... the notion of perceived failure of blacks to follow authoritative commands given by their white de facto owners. This rational provides justification to kill, when interpreted on the basis of *"Resisting the Master"*.

~ *Courtesy of Jim Morin @MorinToon* ~

On the basis of "PROPERTY OWNERSHIP", *"perceived disobedience"* by the police justifies the *"Right to Kill"*, just as it did during slavery when the plantation overseers and slave handlers were policing the slaves. This would suggest that even today all Black People are viewed as *"de facto property of White People"* in the minds of Whites and should be treated as "PROPERTY".

The *"Casual Killing Act"* received national exposure during the airing of *"Slavery and the Making of America"*, Thirteen/WNET New York on PBS.org...

"The Casual Killing Act"

Act of the Commonwealth of Virginia 1669 Cited in William Walter Henning. THE STATUTES AT LARGE; BEING A COLLECTION OF ALL THE LAWS OF VIRGINIA, FROM THE FIRST SESSION OF THE LEGISLATURE IN THE YEAR 1619. vols I and II. (New York: R & W & G Bartow, 1823)

DOCUMENT DESCRIPTION:

Overseers liberally applied violent punishments such as whippings to slaves they perceived to be transgressive. **This 1669 act declared that, should a slave be killed as a result of extreme punishment, the master should not face charges for the murder**.

TRANSCRIPT:

October 1669
Act I, 2:270
Charles II, King of England

An act about the casual killing of slaves.

WHEREAS the only law in force for the punishment of refractory servants (a) **resisting their master**, mistress or overseer cannot be inflicted upon negroes, nor the obstinacy of many of them by other than violent means to suppress, Be it enacted and declared by this grand assembly, **if any slave resist his master** (or other by his masters order correcting him) **and by the extremity of the correction should chance to die, that his death shall not be accounted felony, but the master** (or that other person appointed by the master to punish him) **be acquitted from molestation, since it cannot be presumed that prepended malice** (which alone makes murder a felony) **should induce any man to destroy his owner's estate.**

THE LACK OF "PUBLIC SENTIMENT" CAN BE…

A "LICENSE TO KILL" IN A RACIST CULTURE!!!

Self-castigation an enemy unto itself!!!

I believe the *apparent loss of public sentiment* among a large majority of American Whites in the 21st century is directly linked to *"self-castigation"* on behalf of younger Black folks who are totally clueless when it comes to the value of *"positive public perception"* in a multi-racial society. The social consequences apply to all African Americans who are struggling to overcome the *"last-class stigma"* that is associated with 246 years of slavery that ending just 150 years ago.

Importance of sticking to who we are as a people!!!

Berry Gordy, Jr. founded Motown Records in 1959 and within 5 years the *"Motown Charm School"* was established to promote a positive and professional Black image among his cadre of entertainers. *Mr. Gordy realized that grooming, poise, and social graces were needed by his artists for "social acceptance" in mainstream America. This was done at a time when structural racism was not constrained by law and camouflaged as it is today.* He understood the critical importance of *"positive public perception"* relative to *"Public Sentiment"*.

> *"Gordy told his artists that they were ambassadors for other African American artists who wanted to break into mainstream music and needed to act like royalty to change the image that was commonly held by the white public at the time."*
>
> *"While not explicitly racist to have an in-house finishing school, it does say a lot about what Berry Gordy at Motown wanted to present to the public."*

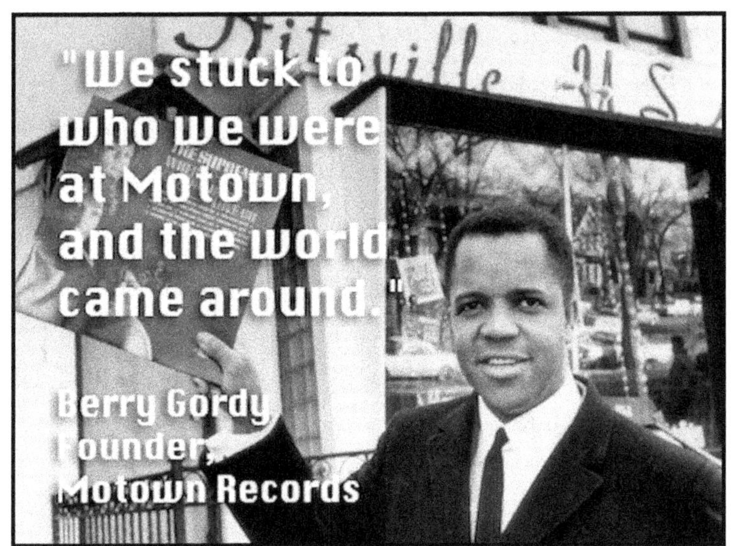

"We stuck to
who we were
at Motown,
and the world
came around."
Berry Gordy
Founder,
Motown Records

*T*o fully understand the phenomenal importance and social impact of *"public sentiment"* upon Black's in America, Barry Gordy's statement should serve as a clarion call and constant reminder to all 21st century African Americans as it relates to our social conduct and personal behavior...

*"We stuck to who we were at Motown
and the world came around."*

*S*adly, the sacrifice and social discipline that was demonstrated by those who paved the way to the freedoms that African Americans enjoy today have been abandoned and ignored by the more recent generations of Black People, wherein the change of course has come at a grave and considerable cost.

*T*his is especially true when it comes to the social assimilation of a minority group of people who were once slaves in a multi-racial society foundered upon racial discrimination against enslaved Africans and their descendants. *"We have abandoned who we were!!!"*

America's double standard toward Blacks!!!

Unfortunately, Blacks receive treatment based upon looks and behavior irrespective of the law. On the basis of historical treatment, we are viewed differently in the American family. Although citizens constitutionally, we are considered *"outsiders"* from a collective standpoint, based upon our slavery orientation into American society.

In fact, history as shown that every immigrant group that entered into America that were not of British descent received extremely harsh and discriminatory treatment. This is true for the *Polish, Italians, Germans, Jews, Asians, Hispanics, and the like.* The harsh and cruel treatment served as a form of initiation in exchange for American citizenship. The hostile and inhumane treatment was endured as a form of hazing for receiving citizenship into the American family. Once initiated, the hazing stops for every ethnic group except African Americans, whom were never intented to receive American citizenship due to slavery. *Black life in America is very similar to running a daily, medieval gauntlet of destruction, wherein millions are permanently damaged and totally destroyed!!!*

For African Americans, group acceptance is determined on a preselected basis that is deemed beneficial to the ruling class and does not equally apply to Blacks; *we are the social, economic, and political exception.* African Americans are yet to be fully integrated into the American family group, resulting in Blacks being judged by a different set of standards.

Consequently, the unfavorable actions and behaviors by those that have been fully accepted into the American family based upon their immigrant status are condoned and viewed as simple mistakes and alleged mental illnesses. Yet, when the identical actions and behaviors are committed by Blacks, we are socially condemned and branded criminals.

So we have to hold ourselves to a higher standard than other ethnic groups in American to avoid the *"negative social consequences"* that apply to us as *"outsiders"*, based upon our entry status into America as *"slaves"*. Unfortunately, history has shown that we cannot conduct ourselves like the immigrant masses that make up the ruling class in America and expect to receive equal justice and fair treatment under laws that were not designed to afford us equal protection.

Positive Image Presentation fuels Public Sentiment!!!

When it comes to *"personal presentation"* as it relates to *conduct, behavior, and dress,* we have to be at our best at all times. If not, *"negative presentation"* becomes a prescription for penalty and retribution for violating the *"social norms"* in American society. One would think that all Americans would be treated fairly and equal under the law, but when it comes to Blacks that is not the case, due to our slavery past. *We are ex-slaves!*

The legal treatment of Blacks is conditional based upon our personal presentation of self and public conduct as a people, relative to matters of *political, social, and economic issues* that are taking place at any given point in time. In essence, when it comes to citizenship we are treated like *"unwanted step children"*. Treatment of Blacks is based upon the ruling class' interpretation and appraisal of our civic and social conduct irrespective of the law.

Younger Blacks must be told by older Blacks that *"sagging"* although covered under the Constitution as a *"freedom of expression"*, is in fact *"indecent exposure"*. When one's underwear is being worn outside of one's trousers, partially exposing one's buttocks to the public, this is without doubt *"indecent exposure"* based upon any measure or standard public conduct.

Negative Image Presentation comes with a cost!!!

"Negative Image Presentation" breeds contempt in White society and causes pain and suffering in every sector of Black society, resulting from *"Black's... castigation of oneself"*.

"Castigation" is defined as... *"the act of being subjected to severe punishment, reproof or criticism"*. Castigation of oneself can cause an individual or group to be judged and penalized by a different set of standards than others in a given society.

"Self-castigation" can result from *"negative image presentation of oneself"*, which damages the *"public perception"* that functions to fuel *"public sentiment"*. Public sentiment has its advantages for a minority class of people, who are *"ex-slaves"* living in a society with a pro-slavery history and a racist past. Public sentiment can be the difference between the *"benefit of doubt"* being rendered by a Grand Jury with a *biased or racist prosecutor, versus being judged in the court of public opinion* where *"reasonable doubt"* is disregarded by a legal system and jury pools that favor exoneration of the guilty parties, while rendering unjust prosecutions upon the victims, *especially when they are Black!!!*

<u>*With public sentiment...*</u>
<u>*casual killing could not exist!!!*</u>

<u>*Without public sentiment...*</u>
<u>*all injustices are possible!!!*</u>

The *"lack of public sentiment"* makes everything legally admissible that fall *"outside of the boundaries of justice"*, including *racial profiling, excessive use of force, police brutality, false arrest, unjustified police homicide, illegal prosecutions and the like, that result in "guilty until proven innocent"* or *"socially condemned until pronounced dead"*.

Becoming a "Property Candidate" is a choice!!!

The unwelcomed *fashion statements, vulgar language,* and *public display of loose fitting behavior* congers up a mental image of Blacks as "<u>PROPERTY CANDIDATES</u>" alongside White People. Our public conduct congers up forgotten memories of our *"<u>slavery past</u>"* in the minds of those whom speak openly of "STATES SECESSION" and relish the idea of turning the clock back to a time wherein <u>*"NIGGER" was deemed legal on the basis of "PERSONAL PROPERTY & PRIVATE OWNERSHIP"*</u>.

Prior to the gears of the slave trade beginning to turn, there were millions of native Africans who never dreamed they would one day awake in a *"Gordon, the slave scenario"*. The indigenous west Africans were viewed as *"easy prey for capture"* based in-part on their scantily dressed appearance and native social habits. <u>*This should serve as a warning!!!*</u>

We desperately need to clean up our act!!!

The "FORBIDDEN TREASURE" of the 21st century free Blacks could be found buried in the hearts and minds of the 17th and 18th century African slaves and late 19th and 20th century Negroes' imagination. Dr. Martin Luther King, Jr. and Malcolm X among others fought and died to uncover that *"forbidden treasure"* and today it is referred to by all as the *"American Dream"!!!*

There is a thin line between *"poverty"* and *"prosperity"* that is quite similar to the thin line between *"dependence"* and *"independence"*. The thin line between *"poverty"* and *"prosperity"* is *"money"*. When all of the money is spent one becomes poor.

The thin line between *"dependence"* and *"independence"* is *"freedom"*. When the *"constitutional freedoms"* of a people are not used wisely, they become *"independence impoverished"* and are placed in a position of becoming the *"mistreated human property"* of those who are free.

Black freedom... A different kind of freedom!!!

Upon performing a careful review of Black history going back to the abolition of slavery it is clear based upon the emergence of Jim Crow Laws and the rise of the Klu Klux Klan that the freedom received by Negroes was a *"DIFFERENT KIND OF FREEDOM"* enjoyed by Whites. The freedom afforded to White and Asian citizens were interlaced with wide ranging liberties that were not afforded to Black American citizens.

In essence, there were *"two American freedoms"*, one for Whites who were truly free and another for Negroes and so-called colored people that came with restrictions, suppression, loss of life, mounting social restraints and economic oppression. The existence of the *"two American freedoms"* began in 1865 at the conclusion of the American Civil War and began to evolve under gradual change with the passage of the Civil Rights Act (1964) and Voting Rights Act (1965).

From 1965 through 2015, Black people have enjoyed 50 years of *"relatively unfettered American freedom"*, when compared to the *"Black Freedom"* of our past. For the past 2½ decades Blacks have been afforded the rare opportunity of constructing a path to "AFRICAN AMERICAN INDEPENDENCE". In hindsight, the first 25 years of freedom from 1965 through 1980 was built on the linear progression of those who came before us, only for a generational shift to occur that would change the focus and direction of our ongoing collective efforts and forward progress as a people.

A new generation in stark contrast to the old!!!

Beginning in the 1980's the actions and behavior of younger Blacks began to change, causing a major shift that would radically redefine the way in which Blacks are viewed in a social context. Up until this point, the earlier generations of Black People bowed their heads in humble acknowledgement of others versus nodding their heads. At the very same time, caps that were traditionally worn facing forward began to be worn facing backwards, signaling a shift in respect for tradition and authority. Interestingly, as nodding heads were going up, the trousers were coming down.

Trousers of Black youth that were traditionally worn waist-high began to sag across the buttocks, imitating prison culture. The embrace of *"thug life"* was ushered in on the backside of earlier, refreshing, and wholesome rap music, representing *"Rhythmic Articulated Poetry"*. Only to descend into gutter-like vulgarity, wherein traditional rap music morphed into *"gangster rap"*, wherein *"nigger" and "bitch"* became the new taglines of twisted notoriety in music, cinema, and unfiltered public conversations.

In historical review, the last 25 of the past 50 years of *"relatively unfettered freedom"* has been spent dismantling the foundational pillars of *"public sentiment"* that provided the safeguards to a long history of continual progress without the constant threat of *"unchecked social reprisal"* by the policing arm of the establishment, while facing ***zero public outcry!!!***

Freedom & public sentiment... Old social currencies!

"Freedom" and *"public sentiment"* are "OLD SOCIAL CURRENCIES" born out of the days of old that are used to *service* and *maintenance* "INDEPENDENCE". *"Freedom"* and *"public sentiment"* are the only social currencies that an individual or group has and only you can determine how it is spent...

BE CAREFUL HOW YOU SPEND IT!!!

Those who are poor in independence become the de facto property of another to do as they choose and this too is a form of *"SLAVERY"*, regardless of the name.

Far too many people interpret a positive change in social, political, and business behavior by old adversaries to mean that the hearts of the people have changed. In effect, what really changed were the laws.

Congress has the authority to legislate laws,

but in the absence of "public sentiment"
it is impossible to... "legislate love."

In fact, the very laws that were written to protect against *tyranny and evil* in a civilized society are used as shields by the *"wantonly evil doers"*. In effect, "THE LAW" is only as good as the people who are meant to enforce it. In the absence of *"public sentiment"* laws simply exist on paper, rather than in the hearts and conscience of those, who by virtue of their silence embrace the horrible injustices, which are known to exist and cause harm to others in a given society.

America's ongoing war with her own people!!!

> *"On Wednesday, after the announcement that NYPD Officer Daniel Pantaleo would not be indicted for killing Eric Garner, the* NAACP's Legal Defense Fund Twitter *posted a series of Tweets naming 76 men and women who were killed in police custody since the 1999 death of Amadou Diallo in New York." {gawker.com}*

On December 3, 2015 *"Huffington Post"* via *"Black Voices"* featured an in-depth report that was posted on *gawker.com* on December 8, 2014. The report detailed an extensive list of "*unarmed people of color*" killed by the police between 1999 and 2014. *The report chronicled a rash of Black killings by White police officers that began in 1999 correlating to a shift in the social behavior of younger Blacks, only to rapidly escalate with the 2008 election of Barack Hussien Obama being the first Black elected to the office of the American Presidency!!!*

Between the years of 1999 and 2007 14 unarmed deaths occurred totaling 1.75% per year, versus 62 unarmed deaths between the years of 2008 and 2014 totaling 10.3% unarmed deaths per year. The rate of unarmed deaths increased by 588.1% and continues to rise at an increasingly alarming rate leading into 2017.

> *Could the election of the first African American President Barack Hussein Obama have triggered the reemergence of an old phenomenon that was allowed to flourish unchecked due to the "loss of public sentiment" festering at its root???*

The following quotes were taken from the article… "*1 Black Man Is Killed Every 28 Hours by Police or Vigilantes: America Is Perpetually at War with Its Own People*". The article was published on May 28, 2013 by Adam Hudson of AlterNet, based upon an aggregate study performed by the Malcolm X Grassroots Movement on the killings of Blacks:

> *"Police officers, security guards, or self-appointed vigilantes extrajudicially killed at least 313 African Americans in 2012 according to a recent study. This means a black person was killed by a security officer every 28 hours. The report notes that it's possible that the real number could be much higher."*
>
> *"Operation Ghetto Storm" explains why such killings occur so often. Current practices of institutional racism have roots in the enslavement of black Africans, whose labor was exploited to build the American capitalist economy, and the genocide of Native Americans.*
>
> *The report points out that in order to maintain the systems of racism, colonialism, and capitalist*

exploitation, the United States maintains a network of "repressive enforcement structures". These structures include the police, FBI, Homeland Security, CIA, Secret Service, prisons, and private security companies, along with mass surveillance and mass incarceration."

President Obama's election prompts secession calls!!!

In 2012, the Los Angeles Times reported that 50 states filed petitions on behalf of their citizens for *"secession"* from the United States of America desiring to form their own sovereign government.

White House receives secession pleas from all 50 states

November 14, 2012
By Danielle Ryan

"WASHINGTON -- What began as a small group of citizens voicing their disappointment with President Obama's victory in last week's presidential election has turned into a plea from hundreds of thousands of citizens to have their states be granted independence from the federal government."

"The White House has now received secession petitions from all 50 states by citizens requesting that the administration *"peacefully grant"* them the opportunity to form their own sovereign government."

A petition drive culminated on November 14, 2012, expressing a desire on behalf of all 50 states to invoke the *"States-Rights Doctrine"* that provides argument for *"nullification of Federal Laws"* under the 10th Amendment of the Constitution. If successful, the Federal Government would have ceased to function as enforcement arm of the United States Constitution.

*W*ithout *"citizenry protection"* under Federal Law, things would revert to individual states being empowered to reinstate the *"Black Codes"* of the Jim Crow Era that restricted the freedom and advancement of African Americans prior to Civil Rights, reducing Blacks to "THE PEOPLE'S PROPERTY".

Property and nigger... Inextricably linked!!!

*H*istorically speaking, the word '*"NIGGER"* when viewed on the basis of *"PROPERTY"* in combination with *"states secession"* and *"sovereign statehood"* creates a potential *"Jim Crow"* and *"Gordon, the slave scenario"*.

"*Gordon, the slave: Harper's Weekly, July 4, 1863*"

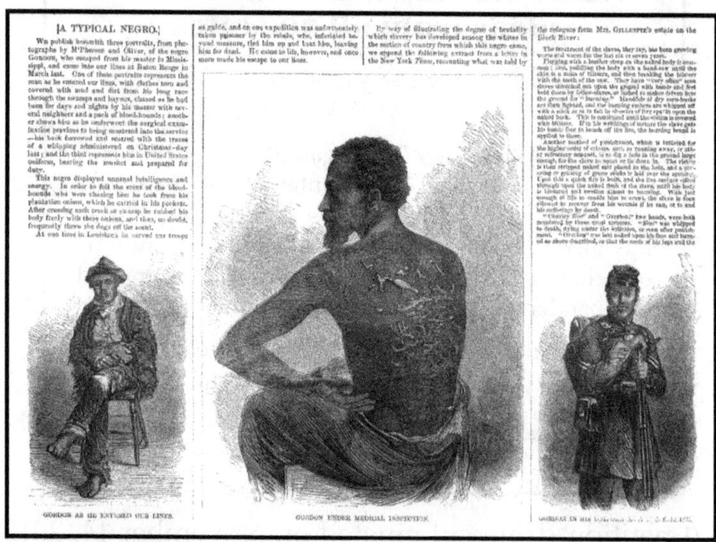

A TYPICAL NEGRO.

We publish herewith three portraits, from photographs by M'Pherson and Oliver, of the negro Gordon, who escaped from his master in Mississippi, and came into our lines at Baton Rouge in March last. One of these portraits represents the man as he entered our lines, with clothes torn and covered with mud and dirt from his long race through the swamps and bayous, chased as he had been for days and nights by his master with several neighbors and a pack of blood-hounds; another shows him as he underwent the surgical examination previous to being mustered into the service—his back furrowed and scarred with the traces of a whipping administered on Christmas-day last; and the third represents him in United States uniform, bearing the musket and prepared for duty.

This negro displayed unusual intelligence and energy. In order to foil the scent of the blood-hounds who were chasing him he took from his plantation onions, which he carried in his pockets. After crossing each creek or swamp he rubbed his body freely with these onions, and thus, no doubt, frequently threw the dogs off the scent.

At one time in Louisiana he served our troops as guide, and on one expedition was unfortunately taken prisoner by the rebels, who, infuriated beyond measure, tied him up and beat him, leaving him for dead. He came to life, however, and once more made his escape to our lines.

By way of illustrating the degree of brutality which slavery has developed among the whites in the section of country from which this negro came, we append the following extract from a letter in the New York *Times*, recounting what was told by the refugees from Mrs. Gillespie's estate on the Black River:

The treatment of the slaves, they say, has been growing worse and worse for the last six or seven years. Flogging with a leather strap on the naked body is common; also, paddling the body with a hand-saw until the skin is a mass of blisters, and then breaking the blisters with the teeth of the saw. They have "very often" seen slaves stretched out upon the ground with hands and feet held down by fellow-slaves, or lashed to stakes driven into the ground for "burning." Handfuls of dry corn-husks are then lighted, and the burning embers are whipped off with a stick so as to fall in showers of fire sparks upon the naked back. This is continued until the victim is covered with blisters. If in his writhings of torture the slave gets his hands free to brush off the fire, the burning brand is applied to them.

Another method of punishment, which is inflicted for the higher order of crimes, such as running away, or other refractory conduct, is to dig a hole in the ground large enough for the slave to squat or lie down in. The victim is then stripped naked and placed in the hole, and a covering or grating of green sticks is laid over the opening. Upon this a quick fire is built, and the live embers sifted through upon the naked flesh of the slave, until his body is blistered and swollen almost to bursting. With just enough of life to enable him to crawl, the slave is then allowed to recover from his wounds if he can, or to end his sufferings by death.

"Charley Slos" and "Overton," two hands, were both murdered by these cruel tortures. "Slos" was whipped to death, dying under the infliction, or soon after punishment. "Overton" was laid naked upon his face and burned as above described, so that the cords of his legs and the

GORDON AS HE ENTERED OUR LINES.

GORDON UNDER MEDICAL INSPECTION.

GORDON IN HIS UNIFORM AS A U.S. SOLDIER.

*T*herefore, the word *"nigger"* has negative value as a *"social currency"* when used in any context. It can only spend in the minds of those (*be they White or Black*), who relish the idea of Black People being in a *"Master - servant"* relationship to White People as their *"state property" or "personal property"*.

In 1705 the State of Virginia relegated *slaves, Native Americans* and *mulattos* to the status of property. So when White People refer to Black People as... *"NIGGER"* and *"NIGGERS"* they are in effect stating that the person or persons they are subjecting to this extremely derogatory and *"racially abusive branding"* are still the de facto *"legal property"* of White People. On a personal level they are asserting themselves as present day *"owner"* and *"Massa"*, issuing out of a foregone era.

When Black People affectionately or unaffectionately refer to themselves as... *"NIGGER"*, *"NIGGA"*, *"NIGGERS"*, and *"NIGGAS"* colloquially, *we* are in effect *"openly inviting actions"* that are deemed utterly offensive. By communicating in this way, we are identifying ourselves with one another on the basis of *"PROPERTY"*, which is clearly denoted by the use of... ***"MY NIGGER"***. This perpetuates a *"last-class image"* that equates all Black People to *"twenty first century slaves" unaware!!!*

The "mismanaged treasure" of the 21st century free Blacks could be found buried in the "chancery outcrop" of the African slaves' imagination, a treasure stemming from the "bedrock of racial inequality" that is known to all Americans as "Freedom"!!!

~ Poetic Reflections ~

Looking Back!!!

Looking Back to See Our Way Forward...

"Great African American Men"

Artist & Contributor : Wishum Gregory

Wishumgregoryart.com

~ End of an Era ~

From Colored freedom to American freedom!!!

In 1955 Rosa Louise McCauley Parks, then 42 years of age took a defiant stand in Montgomery, Alabama, during a period in American history when Black People, the so-called *"Negroes" (previously deemed three-fifths of a human being and barred Constitutional rights as citizens)* were treated as *"last class citizens"* and denied equal treatment in the areas of human rights, jobs, housing, education, and civil rights.

There were segregated communities, segregated schools, hotels, theaters, parks, beaches, lunch counters, government buildings, department stores, churches, and military units. All public facilities were fitted with separate restrooms and water fountains with posted signs labeled *"Colored"* and *"White Only"*, requiring back door access for Negroes. The mass transit, public venues, and shared public facilities had separate seating areas for Whites and Blacks.

There were two sets of standards for education, school books, jobs, and wages, in addition to a social protocol that required Negroes to enter all public facilities and public transit units through the rear and ride in the back of the buses in the *"Colored Section"*.

*R*osa Park's courageous stand signaled the beginning to an end for the legalized racial injustices imposed upon Black people that existed in the United States throughout American history up until the 1960s. A simple yet courageous act by Rosa Parks would transform the ongoing Human Rights Movement into the Civil Rights Movement of the 1950's and 60s. Her refusal to surrender her seat to a White man once the *"White Section"* was filled provided the catalyst for the Civil Rights Legislation of 1964.

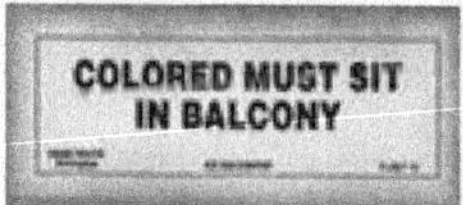

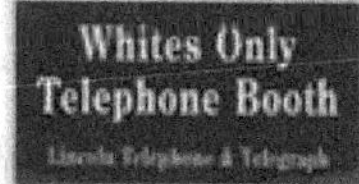

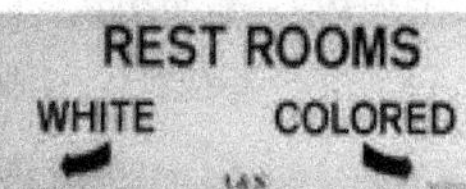

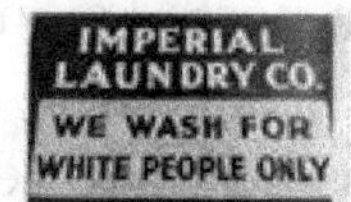

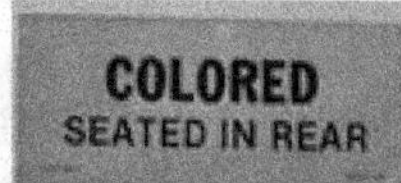

~ Her Name is Rosa ~

Elevating the "Negro"...
America's second class citizen!

There she sits with honor and dignity,
proudly poised at the very front of the bus…
Seated in an area she could not have legally sat,
during the early years of her youth.

She sits tall, frame erect, chin up, eyes focused…
with little to no concern for the White world
that surrounds her, as she reflects upon
the racial difficulties confronting the Negro people...

And the bus rolls on...

"Next stop... Ann Street".
"Driver! Driver! I need a transfer..."
"Sir..., can you help me please?"
"Ma'am... excuse me ma'am...,"
"I'm trying to get through!"

And the bus rolls on...

Seated to the left and right of her...
are two Caucasian females,
both exchanging occasional stares,
while gazing profusely at Rosa as if
they are watching *"Queen For A Day"*
through rose colored tinted glasses.

And the bus rolls on...

The younger of the two women
appear to be in her late twenties,
or early thirties...

She has a thin build,
sandy blonde hair and hazel green eyes.
She is neatly dressed,
in simple plain clothing,
with head hung high,

having little of anything to say to anyone.

On the other side…
in breathing distance of Rosa,
is a slightly wrinkled, late to middle-aged,
blue eyed brunette.

She is wearing a lightly soiled,
slightly wrinkled waitress uniform.
She is reading *"Dear Abby"* aloud,
while chewing gum and chuckling to herself,
after finishing every single line.

Seated across from them...
are three young adult Negroes;
two females and one male.

The females are openly competing
to be whiter than the Whites...
both speaking in inflationary language
that only they could possibly understand,
while debating aloud about the content
of their newly found character.

And the bus rolls on...

"Next stop... Fairview Avenue..."
"Everyone standing, please move back
toward the rear of the bus"!

The stop light changes...
everyone is swayed by the bus' untimely jolt...
but Rosa is firmly planted,
like a tree by a river that dare not be moved.

And the bus rolls on...

As soon as the bus approaches its next stop...
the lighter skinned female of the two Negro girls

spoke to the other female in a rather loud voice,
accompanied by a telling tone...

*"I kind of liked the brother at first girl, that is...
until he began with the Black this and White that,
he's much too radical and ghetto for me girl".*

And the bus rolls on...

In the silence of a whisper,
as the bus passes *"The Greasy Spoon Café"...*
James Brown can be heard singing...

*"Play it loud, I'm Black and I'm proud...",
"Get an education or you might as well be dead..."*

For just a moment the passengers are caught up
in a sound track of silence, until... the other "sister"
retorted in an extremely high-pitched voice...

*"You're just jealous of the brother's Blackness
and his militant attitude toward the struggle."
"And you, you're just an Aunt Jemima and a phony"!*

And the bus rolls on...

The bus methodically rocks and reels
as it jerks and screeches to a stop...
signaling an end to another long day's journey.

The motion causes the blonde and brunette
to press their tense bodies against Rosa's,
just as they scrambled to gather themselves,
suggesting the unwanted contact, although brief...
had never really happened.

Never the less, Rosa maintains her posture
and strengthens her composure as if to say...

"... I am the only person on this bus

and nobody is seated next to me".

The Black bus driver shouts aloud!

"End of the line..."
"End of the line..."

In an effort to break the humdrum of silence
garnered by a very long and overcrowded trip,
the brunette laughs aloud uncontrollably,
as she closes the cover of her *"Dear Abby"*,
as if to say...

"This bus is mine!!!
Everybody riding on it belongs to me,
including that underpaid black ass nigger driver"!

While at the same time,
Rosa's every action speaks volumes
of how she views the White world around her.

Again the bus driver shouts...

"End of the line..."
"End of the line..."

~ A tribute to Rosa Parks ~

Rosa Park's courageous stand,
that was taken on December 1, 1955
by not getting up from her "second class"
designated seat sent an astounding signal to
the Negro opposition in America.

A resounding message was heard by those
who failed to realize that their racially oppressive
vehicle of segregation had arrived at the end of
the line on that fateful and historical day
in Montgomery, Alabama!

Rosa…

We the twenty-first century Blacks
all across this land salute your stand.

We honor you for being an ambassador of
courage in the ongoing struggle against
segregation and racism in America, that
sent shockwaves around the world!

Your presence will be missed,
but your legacy will remain
as an enduring symbol for every
Black American that come after you.

Those of us today that sit on the front seats
of buses, trains, airplanes, cruise ships, spaceships
and numerous executive boards of America's
largest corporations, while being addressed as "African
Americans" applaud your defiant stand.

Your "dignified repudiation" begs the question…

How could one seemingly powerless,
"so-called" colored female's defiant stand ignite
the fire that changed the entire racial equation in
America, just by sitting down and refusing to get up?

Rosa… Your courageous stand afforded an entire race
of people the opportunity to be seated in high places!!!

Who would have believed that your act
of resistance would have opened the door for
Barack Hussein Obama , a "person of color" to
sit behind the Commander and Chief's desk in the
oval office of the White House as the 44th President of
the United States of America just two generations later.

We honor your legacy and salute your courage!

~ Martin's Dream ~

"Fly with me..."

What could it be, said he...
would you please tell me?

What could be more repelling,
than a sunflower...
that seeded the native source
of all human breaths of life.

One that does not bloom
or blossom anymore...

Imagine a bird...
that does not sing,
nor spread its wings...
before it dies.

He said...
Listen with tears,
and you shall hear...
The sounds...
of your people crying.

Crying out for the wants...
and needs...
of a new belonging.

Crying out for the need to "BE"!
To "be" *independent...*
To "be" *happy...*
To "be" *free...*

To "be" non-subjected,
to the agonizing toils...
of tranquil futility,

while chasing western mirages...
of hopeless delusion.

Yes listen, and you too will hear...
their low chatters, vain whispers,
and desperate outcries,
innocently assessing…
the evil notions surrounding them.

Notions accompanied by...
gesturing sighs of uncertainty,
that are screaming from behind,
human walls of shallow doubt.

For some... the fleeting thoughts,
of a better tomorrow.
For others... the echoes and resounding tremors,
of a post hypnotic success.

While the non-surrendering calls to mend...
the *social, economic* and *political frustrations,*
go unanswered.

He said...
Dear little flower, please tell me...
When will you breathe the air of Blackness…
where the "*Black Birds of Freedom*" sing?

"*I HAVE OVERCOME!!!*"

Living in a world where beautiful birds...
are caged and enslaved;
being made to believe,
they do not have wings to fly.

Living a life of steadfast existence...
where birds of song,
are rendered unto desert flowers.

Never intended to sing...
nor stretch their wings and fly...

Yes fly... to fly as high as they please...
above the clouds of *"so-called"* ethnic impurities,
joyfully singing as they flee.

Martin said...
Come little birds and fly with me!

~ *Martin Luther King, Jr.* ~

"If you can't fly, run.
If you can't run, walk.
If you can't walk, crawl.
But by all means, keep moving."

March 31, 1956

~ Black Like Me ~

From the *"Cradle of Civilization"*,
GOD formed the original nation,
whom birthed a family...
in a faraway land,
with descendants as numerous
as grains of sand.

A more beautiful place
you shall never see
having *"knowledge"* and *"truth"*
grown on a family tree.

I will forever believe
they looked just like me.

They were lords of peace,
reality and truth,
sustained by nature
in her fullness of youth.

But something happened
only God knows where
that changed the story
from *"dark"* to *"fair"*.

It's like our Lord and brother,
once said to thee
"Eli... Eli... la'ma sa-bath' tha-ni".

My God, my God, why has thou forsaken me?

Long before "mankind" existed,
there was just man... "The Black Man".
Archeological and genetic research has proven that
the African is the "ethnic trunk" of "Humanity's Tree".

~ Book Ends ~

Here I sit...
a closed book behind a wall,
the oldest, longest, strongest, informative...
one of the most knowledgeable of them all.

A book of flesh...
not held by hands nor embraced by grace,
discarded and disregarded,
by the entire human race.

A book not studied nor read in depth...
seldom placed high on the human shelf,
unknown for my arsenal,
of immeasurable wealth.

For centuries I have sat...
behind a human wall of pain,
expressing pages of righteous indignation,
intermingled with shame.

Chapter...
by chapter...
my native name,
has been changed.

"Children of Alkebu..."
Ethiopian, African, *"nigger you"*
Colored, Negro, Black...
now African American too.

I am the story of Blackness...
transcribed in layers of blue.
Color blue... for the blues!
Color black... for the hue!

Yes hue... hue like in hu-man,

I am "THE FIRST" of us all,
adorned as first fruit,
from the Master's roll call.

I am the elder of humanity,
created from native virgin soil;
I am the *"Ancient-Namer"* of all things,
I am "*The Adam & Eve*" of us all.

By the Greeks I was called the Autochthones,
"One who sprung from the soil itself",
"The very first of all men..."
a book, cast down from its shelf.

Book Ends...

Prior to the advent of writing,
information was mentally stored
and disseminated by chosen people
whom were known as "oracles".

Oracles were "human books of person"
that functioned as encyclopedias of heritage.
They transmitted historical knowledge
and information to the passing generations.

This process was known as "Oral Tradition".
In the village or ghetto there were three oracles...
The parents, the teachers, and the preachers...
These were the three voices that we could hear...
They provided the foundation, path, and guidance.

Today there is only one voice that is heard in the village...
That being the voice of the Rapper...
The Rapper is the oracle, "the voice" the youth can hear.
When it comes to collective cultural correction,
we must rediscover the three oracles within ourselves!!!

~ A Burnt Face People ~

"Ethios Ops..."

Like our distant forefathers...
the ancient Ethiopians,
we have a lot to give.

Like our Egyptian ancestors...
the founding fathers of civilization,
we are blessed with skills to build.

We are the very first people...
the tree trunk of nations...
we are the original kingdom people,
grafted out of a chosen generation.

"Ethios" as in burnt...
"Ops" as in face...
Ethiopians are people of color,
who put the *"hue"* in *"Human Race"!*

"I am black, but comely..."
King Solomon wrote,
"the hair of his head was like pure wool..."
a description of Jesus, the Prophet Daniel spoke.

"My people are destroyed for lack of knowledge"...
Prophet Hosea decreed,
"because thou hast rejected knowledge,
I will also reject thee..."

Black Man...
in all thy knowing...
seek to know thyself!

Ethiopians... the so-called "colored people"...
blessed of God to have melanin in the walls of their skin!!!

~ History vs. His-Story ~

Biased versions…
of a story told,
truth taxed, waxed, relaxed
from the precolonial days of old.

From beneath the veil
and behind the masks,
screaming voices cry out
from millenniums past.

Balance being spoken
in various forms,
raising humanity's brow
causing subtle alarm.

Art, pictographs, folklore,
hieroglyphics, books and scrolls...
knowledge of the ancients...
telling a story untold.

The Arts, Sciences, Religion
and Philosophy ascribed to the Greeks,
were extracted from the writings
and teachings of Egyptian priests.

If the truth be known
of our African ancestors due,
the legacy of CIVILIZATION...
belongs to you.

Your story...
The African story...
The maiden, mother, and midwife...
of all stories!

~ The Hebejebe Man ~

"The people who make the other people nervous!"

A long, long time ago,
deep within the heart of Alkebu-lan;
there lived a native boy,
who would become the Hebejebe Man.

I can see him now,
building pyramids in the sand;
I can see him centuries earlier,
with his spear and shield in hand.

I can see him day by day,
mapping the stars beneath the sky;
it was he who created the calendar,
that today we all live by.

I can see him carving the magnificent sphinx,
beneath the light of the Horus Eye.
I can see him flying his chariot,
far above the eastern sky.

I can see him dressing the River Nile,
as only an African Pharaoh can.
I can see him walking with GOD,
throughout the Motherland.

I can see an Ethiopian Kid,
the original African;
he was first to perform brain surgery,
he invented medicine.

It was he who developed law,
science and astronomy;
he mastered the laws of physics,
and was first to sail the sea.

Very early he invented *"papyrus"* for writing,
for he knew that writing was key;
he authored one of man's earliest books *(Egyptian bible),*
he created geometry.

Oh what a boy...
Oh what a man...
now he's just,
the Hebejebe Man!

Well... on one lone summer's day,
while wrestling lions in the sand;
he was captured and shipped to America,
never to return again.

Upon being put on the boats,
he was shackled, chained, and locked;
within minutes after he got off,
he was sold on the auction block.

He wore a dismal smile...
on faces black, then brown, then tan;
every day he would cry out aloud,
"Lord... please take me home again".

He was very highly civilized,
knowing GOD before most men could;
but as the story would have it,
he's treated like old *"dead wood".*

And I'm here to tell you,
he's great by any name;
but anytime things go wrong,
he's made to bear the blame.

I can hear the other people screaming,
with King James Bibles open in hand;

"you see... we don't have to prove he did it",
he's just a Hebejebe Man.

Oh what a boy...
Oh what a man...
now he's just,
the Hebejebe Man!

He's the world's greatest fighter,
in and out of the ring;
but he's never meant to win,
he's the Hebejebe Man.

He deserves the right as all men,
to be rewarded in his life;
but he's always made to wait,
and pay a higher price.

He wins the highest medals,
on track, field and land;
but he's treated like a nobody,
he's the Hebejebe Man.

I can see him now... fighting America's wars,
like Iraq, Afghanistan and Vietnam;
but he's treated with disrespect,
he's the Hebejebe Man.

Even though belittled...
he stands as big as life;
he's fighting for tomorrow,
he's struggling to save his life.

He does all within his power,
striving to be the best he can;
but it doesn't really matter,
for he's the Hebejebe Man.

Oh what a boy...
Oh what a man...
now he's just,
the Hebejebe Man!

He's sometimes short...
He's sometimes tall...
He sometimes try,
to be king of us all.

He's sometimes fat,
as big as a band;
if you look real hard,
you'll see the Hebejebe Man.

He wears a big nose,
but sometimes not;
he comes in many shades,
of various stock.

He has *"hair like lamb's wool"*
and *"feet like burnished bronze"* like Jesus;
He's a child of GOD,

he's a firm believer.

In Jamaica he wears dreadlocks,
in America sometimes a curl;
for millenniums he's worn the afro,
around and around the world.

Today he may be a bagman,
Supreme Court Justice, Lawyer, or Priest;
the President of the United States of America,
or simply sleeping on the street.

If you look in the mirror,
you may see him today;
he could be driving a Rolls Royce,
or riding the subway.

He finally grown old,
he's now tired and gray;
but don't count him out,
for he's here to stay.

So here the story,
and follow the clues;
for the person you find,
just maybe...

You!

Hebejebes imply uneasiness or nervousness,
being brought upon people…

We are the people who make the other people nervous...
The "nervous people" are those who initially kidnapped,
stole, and brought us to the Americas against our will,
in the aftermath of our unfortunate discovery!!!

~ Shipwrecked ~

"We... The people!!!"

On the ships and boats of many,
to the American continent our forefathers came,
from diverse nations and cultures,
on seafaring vessels from faraway lands.

We are all in the same boat!

Republicans, Democrats, Independents,
Libertarians, political dissenters alike,
riding shifting waves of global economics,
political malfeasance and relentless terrorist attacks.

We are all in the same boat!

Native Americans, Asians, Europeans,
African Americans, Latin Americans among many,
burdened with immorality, injustices, and poverty,
in a nation of laws favoring the rich and plenty.

We are all in the same boat!

"Where do we go from here?"
In 1967, I heard a beacon's resounding call...
jarring the walls of America's social consciousness,
for her to awake and embrace us all.

We are all in the same boat!

Abe Lincoln, JFK, RFK, MLK, Malcolm X, and others...
their lives sacrificed for you and me,
champions of social justice, martyred...
forcing America to *"truly"* be the land of the free.

We are all in the same boat!

Imagine all Americans in a boat... sinking,

with ores being used for weapons rather than tools,
the wise would perish by destructive acts of the
ignorant, while the bigots are fighting like fools.

We are all in the same boat!

America is a multi-cultured nation,
unlike Russia, North Korea, China, and Iran,
if we continue to discount our national diversity,
the monolithic nations will sift us like sand.

We are all in the same boat!

On June 16, 1858 Senator Abraham Lincoln,
the future American Civil War President stated...
"A house divided against itself cannot stand."

~ Acirema ~

America, America...
powerful and grand,
where *"patriots"* and *"martyrs"*
have bloodied the land.

You are the land of the free,
the home of the brave,
where the greatest of minds
lay slain and enslaved.

Rembrandt the artist
was not as great as you,
at painting success
in shades of blue.

Leonardo da Vinci
at the height of his fame,
could not have painted
"AMERICAN SLAVERY"...
and given it a name.

America, America...
oh shining star,
examine yourself
and know who you are.

Because we *"the people"*,
We the *"American people"*,
We the *"African American people"*,
We love you... so very, very much.

America is a 500 years plus social experiment...
wherein the native people and culture was destroyed
and supplanted with foreigners from all races and lands.

~ Uhuru ~

"Freedom in Swahili..."

Beautiful, dutiful maiden,
constructing a coffin a dust;
cushioned with bewilderment,
slickery and tricks.

Oil, diamonds,
copper and gold;
filling eroded cracks,
in a belligerent soul.

Angola, Congo,
Rhodesia, Sudan;
recounting history,
beneath Sahara sands.

Another man's freedom,
is not your own...
Each and every man,
must search out his own path!!!

~ Ain't I Hot ~

"For whom the freedom bell tolled…"

Cracks in duh melt'n pot and ain't I hot?
Ain't I hot? Ain't I hot? I's hot as hell!
Dats what I said! Yeh, dats what I said!
Cause I's hot as hell!

But ole boss he's auh keepin dis-shihen so thick,
dat I kan'h melt.
But like Massa said… if I pray hard enuff,
fuh muh pie in duh sky, dis-shihen go'n thin foe I die.

Den I's go'n buy me a hossy and buggee, shinee black,
fetch me a pretty littie sugar dumplin and lay back.
Dats what I said... Yeh, dats what I said!
Cause I's hot as hell!

Ya see..
I's go'n overcome dees candy coated clouds,
created by sundust smiles;
dats reflect'n the heavens
of uh fools desire.

An ain't I hot? Ain't I hot?
I's hot as hell! Dats what I said.
Yeh, dats what I said! Dats what I said.
Cause I's hot as hell!

Ya see mamma done wurk 40 yeahs,
scrubbin lilly white floes;
sum'um Doctor Schriber says,
she ain't spos'd to do no moe.

Jus to brang me up
on dis tuff tit,

where dees udduh dat-gum folks
doh'n even hit a lick.

An ain't I hot? Ain't I hot?
I's hot as hell! Dats what I said!
Yeh, dats what I said! Dats what I said!
Cause I's hot as hell!

Ya see… ole pop got lynched,
den all me uncles got throwed in jail;
left mamma and duh ress of us,
back henh ketchen hell.

Junior went off to duh siva war
an died of starvation an belly rot,
an now mamma's dead
an I's all we's got.

And ain't I hot? Ain't I hot?
I's hot as hell! Dats what I said!
Yeh, dats right! Dats what I said!
Cause I's hot as hell!

But be-en hot don-h feed...
me, Bay, Jig, Dillie, Junya, Maggie and Joe,
but I's duh man urv da house,
an dat I know.

I's fit-teen yeahs old,
no job, no trade,
but don't you damn dare,
call me no slave.

Cause afta I hit jus a few moe licks,
I's gon-h hav my merikan dream;
I's gon-h be hossy and buggee hard,
I's gon-h be hossy and buggee mean.

But wait, sebdy yeahs done passed…
an I's donh hav enni than dat I's ever wanted;
I's ain't happy, I's ain't satified,
an I's sho ain't free.

I's fuh got all uh bout duh hossy,
I's fuh got all uh bout duh buggee,
an sugar dumplin and da hole world
dun all fuh got uh bout me!

Fuh dis cause I's hot! I's vary hot!
Dats right, I's hot… Dats what I said!
Cause I's on fire for Colored freedom,
an I's stremely hot as hell!

Illiteracy and lack of basic education
was commonplace during and after slavery.

Intellectual knowledge was reserved for "Whites Only";
Blacks were told and encouraged to work with their hands.

It was against the rules for Blacks to exhibit intelligence;
"Openly intelligent Blacks" were labelled "smart niggers".

"Book learning" was frowned upon as if it were a crime;
Books, money, and freedom were deemed contraband!!!

Under the "Jim Crow Rules" of yesterday,
"Ignorance" was a guaranteed recipe for failure.

But for all Black People today…
when it comes to "Ignorance"
and the "lack of basic education",
there is no excuse!!!

"If you think education is expensive… Try ignorance"!!!

~ Case Quarter ~

"British colonial slavery remembered…"

Pennies, nickels, dimes...
Oh Lordie!
Been freed a hunderd yeahs
tain't gotta case quarter.

Been workin wit me hands
since duh Lord knows when;
scrapen hen'h and yonder
fuh dem deir paper thins.

Been livin in duh *"git out"*
for most all me days;
wit little ti' no edication
I's simply a slave.

You see… Old Abe's emancipation
is just freedom by name,
cause freedom tain't freedom
wit no economical gain.

Pennies, nickels, dimes...
Oh Lordie!
When will I ever,
git a case quarter?

From duh yeah 1619
up through June 19, 1865,
I's wus never paid a penny
I's felt lucky to be alive.

From June 20, 1865…
till duh Lord knows when,
I's dun scraped pennies, nickels, den dimes,
den back to pennies agin.

I's now three scores and ten
I's at duh end of my life,
Wit out a lick of inheritance
not even a tithe.

I's simply do what I's told
telling questions I ask not,
I's at duh end of my road,
I's back on duh block.

Tain't gotta case quarter!

*There is a tremendous difference
between "capable" and "able".
Capable is having the **capital**
to fund what you are **able** to do.*

*Don't be misled by the book definition...
The wealthy slave masters were capable!
The penniless slaves were able!
Ability without capital is the poor man's curse!*

*Abe is on the darkest money...
Abe is on the least valued money...
Abe is looking in a different direction...
Abraham Lincoln had a different vision...*

*Abe went against the grain, freeing the slaves...
Unfortunately, Abe's conviction cost him his life...*

*The cost of freedom is expensive...
Blacks were never meant to be free...
Your freedom is your best currency...*

~ MBI ~

"A Mighty Big Inheritance..."

Mighty Big Inheritance...
that's the name of the game;
only prescribed for Massa's children...
just whose the blame?

Legacy of legacies,
an extension of self,
with a slavery mentality,
there's nothing left.

Nearly 400 years,
nothing has changed.
Mighty Big Inheritance...
Japheth's posterity gain.

~ Genesis Chapter 9, verse 27 ~

"God shall enlarge Japheth,
and he shall live in the tents of Shem;
and Canaan shall be his servant."

Japheth is the father of the Europeans,
Shem is the father of the Semites,
Ham is the father of the Africans; Ham had "Four Sons"!

Mizraim - Egypt, Phut – Libya, Canaan – Palestine...
We are not descendants of Canaan, but Cush the Ethiopian!

Many have misinterpreted this biblical prophecy
to apply to the enslavement of Blacks in America.
We were not cursed to be slaves with "bondage mentalities"!

~ Muted Drum ~

"Native Ethnicity Lost..."

Why do you hate me?

You have *raped* me!
You have *robbed* me!
You have *hung* me!
You have *starved* me!

Is it something that I have done?

You have *oppressed* me.
You have *deployed* me.
You have *exploited* me.
You have *ignored* me.

You have treated me as no one!

You have destroyed my *history...*
You have destroyed my *tongue...*
You have destroyed my *family...*
You have destroyed my *young...*

My ethnicity and cultural identity
has been systematically erased...
My life, my life... a dramatic tragedy,
transformed from riches to ruin.

Only the starving fool
awaits the crow,
to give back the seeds
that it has eaten!!!

~ Babylon ~

Lost ties... weeping eyes,
chains of bondage in disguise.
meek flesh melting... melting fast,
melting like hot wax on charcoal bones
avenging the wrath of the rich man's throne.

Fun, folly, drink and play
celebrating scores of yesterday.

But nobody cares to hear!!!

Eyes... brown, blue, gray and green
witnessing things they've never dreamed.
Lips thin... thick..., moving super slick,
while our lives flow like wine,
free of purpose and free of time.

Making our children drunk for the world,
while drowning them in
empty promises of yesterday.

But nobody cares to hear!!!

While living in a world
filled with misery and fear,
the fears of what was...
shaping the miseries of what is.

But nobody cares to hear!!!

He that has an ear to hear,
let him hear!!!

~ What's Your Name? ~

Shackles and chains
crowning your brain,
iron or gold
they are still the same.

Yo! Black Man...
What's your name?

You are first for slavery...
last for fame,
in the fields of Mississippi
or on crack cocaine.

Yo! Black Man...
What's your name?

You are servants of servants
from the Motherland,
intertwined in a lie
from the *"Massa Plan"*.

Yo! Black Man...
What's your name?

You were "*Children of Alkebu*"
prior to Egyptian worship of the sun god *"Ra"*,
You descended from Alkebu-lan kings
before *"Christianity"* and Muslims praise of *"Allah"*.

You are *"the subject"* of signs and wonders,
issuing from ancient legacies long overdue;
You have been burdened with hardship
and strife... your whole life through.

You are *"sons of God"*,
enslaved by *"children of man"*,

unwilling disciples of *"his-story"*...
being labelled *"niggers"* in a foreign land.

Yo! Black Man...
What's your name?

Your lineage precedes the *"Black Madonna"*,
the Egyptian's Virgin Mother *"Isis"*,
You are the ancestors and descendants
to *"Osiris"* and his God Child *"Horus"*.

You are of the bloodline of *"Imhotep"*
the *"first renaissance man"* whom preceded the Psalms,
the authentic "FATHER OF MEDICINE"
and *"MASTER OF ARCHITECTURAL CHARM"*.

Listen up Black Man...
for knowledge and truth,
learn the *"knowledge of self"*
for "YOUR STORY" is true.

You were "*Children of Alkebu*"
prior to Egyptian worship of the sun god *"Ra"*,
You descended from Alkebu-lan kings
before *"Christianity"* and Muslims praise of *"Allah"*.

"Alkebu-lan"... earliest reference to the Motherland.
You are the "*Children of Alkebu*"...
Your self-appointed name.

Names are extremely and vitally important...
so much so that man's first God-given duty
was to assign names to all of the animals.

If everyone were to introduce themselves
and practice calling one another by name,
we would be less likely to offend and degrade,
by calling one another racial slurs and other things!!!

~ Liberation ~

"Freedom & Truth..."

Define yourself,
if nothing else;
never be told,
what you can be.

Seek... to know who you are,
in relationship to where you are;
it is only then,
that one becomes free!

Freedom begins in the mind...
with the knowledge of "one's own truth"...

There are three indelible truths...

"Personal truth" is the knowledge of one's total experience!!!

"Collective truth" is the knowledge of a group's total experience shared among its people!!!

"Divine truth" is the knowledge of total experience from the beginning of Creation!!!

Experience becomes truth, when that "experience" is justified on the basis of "study". Study to know your personal, collective, and "Divine truth"... and "the truth" shall make you free!

~ Wismatic Gesture ~

People that continuously walk,
forever watching their feet;
blindly trip over the mistakes of others,
that contribute to their defeat.

Rough roads are seldom traveled,
discouraging bumps they do possess,
pioneers are victims of sacrifice,
as they journey to greet success.

Hold your head high...
Reach for the sky...
No missed steps...
Avoid the *"Big Lie"*...

One critical step at a time!!!

Listen up, know and do...
"To thine own self be true"

~ Orphans ~

Individually as a group, we stand alone…
striving to succeed on our very own;
lacking *"self-knowledge"* inside our heads,
unprepared for the struggles that lie ahead.

It's going to take diligent study, work and time…
to repair the damage that slavery did to our minds;
"VIRTUAL COLONY" holds the key to what we seek,
in order for our lives and journey to be complete.

Every ethnic group other than Blacks,
operate on the basis of a "Self-Imposed Colonial Code".

The Colonial Code is a "universal formula"
that employs ethnic unity, economic independence,
and political power, which produces "ethnic prosperity".

All ethnic groups employ this formula.
Sadly, Black People are the notable exception.
We have to restore our cultural roots of ethnicity,
that ties us together as a group; others cannot do it for us.

Virtual Colony enables a group of people to live apart
due to integration, yet think together and function as one!!!

~ Devolution versus Re.. Evolution ~

"Rediscovery... A vital necessity!!!"

I have seen the carnage of devolution...
in the hearts, souls, and minds of many,
with blood running angrily and thick,
as it pumps and swells in the loins of my people.

I have witnessed devolution...
in funky X-rated apartment buildings,
those solitary urban confinements,
steeped with rent that caresses the moon.

I have felt the sting of devolution...
in the back alleys of run down city streets,
where my people sleep on cardboard boxes for beds,
and use the body heat of others as human furnaces.

I have inhaled the stench of devolution...
from the slime of sewer rats as they freely feed
upon the breast of Black mothers, and have sadly
watched as they sharpen their menacing teeth on the
finger nails and toe nails of Black infants.

I have tasted the vomit of devolution...
in the tin pans and gutter troughs of my ancestors,
as they were being swiftly emptied... yes emptied...
even before being filled... with the indelicacies of
daily slop.

And I have heard tales of devolution...
in the rumblings of the minds of those,
whom expunge their consciousness with the
socially prescribed antidote of drugs, simply because
they are no longer able to dream, nor cope.

I am weakened by the echoes of devolution...

screaming out from the backdrop of drums muted.

Drums that are no longer able to reverberate, tremble, or beat, silenced by centuries of beating oppression in a new world order.

Oppression... springing, regenerating and leaping forth, resounding from the chatter and tatter of shattered huts of non-walled villages in the motherland, that are streaming with poverty, disease, deafening sighs and rumors of revolt.

I am continually touched by devolution...
at the hands of those who would carelessly fondle
my life's story and mishandle my future with
callused hands of malice and reckless forethought.

I am a *"Counter-Re_evolutionary"* in a *"Re_evolutionary world"*;
One who believes that radicalism breeds transition,
in a world of stagnation and desolation, where
"predators of mankind" seek to make me their prey.

"Devolution" is the return to an earlier and usually worst state of condition, wherein one degenerates by moving backwards!!!

"Re_evolution" is a process of continual change from a lower, simpler, or worse state to a higher, more complex, or better state, only to be compelled to restart again and again and again. One appears in practice to be moving forward, but when viewed from the vantage point of progress, one is actually standing still!!!

"Counter-re_evolution" produces non-surrender of social consciousness, acted upon by necessary and appropriate means, when "devolution" and "re.. evolution" are the only options!!!

~ Wanted Dead or Alive ~

"A people lost in translation…"

How could you have sold us
and not have even told us?
You should have explained that the Europeans…
forced purchased, kidnapped and stole us.

Did anyone make it back
to tell you the horrible stories,
of the rapes, castrations, amputations,
lynchings and millions upon millions buried?

But they didn't, because they couldn't,
and we thought you didn't care…
We were told you were counting your blood money
and enjoying the mountains upon mountains of wares.

They tried to change our minds
of how we should feel about you,
but we dug, and dug, and dug,
until we learned the stories were untrue.

We know that you were forced to sell your family,
it wasn't just to acquire money and stuff;
sadly the primitive military power of the Motherland
just wasn't strong enough?

Stop grieving over the millions upon millions lost!
Stop drowning yourself in guilt, agony and tears!
We know that you were not responsible…
for what happened, over the past 570 years.

Even the hoards of ivory, diamonds, silver, copper
and gold couldn't satisfy the European slavers…
who came to enslave your people
and torture your soul.

They say we are guilty of romanticism,
but it is in *"YOU"* that we have survived...
We are among the best of your national treasure!
We love you... *"wanted dead or alive"!*

No longer *"niggers"*,
the legal property of another.
We have survived the worst of the hatred and abuse,
to become *"African American"* sisters and brothers!

Mother Africa...
We are still your children,
and you are our ancestral home.
Home is where family is!!!

~ W. M. Ds. ~

Defenseless souls dying...
innocent lives shattered, crippled and torn;
caught up in a world of vicious spin,
justifying illegal wars going on.

"Weapons of Mass Destruction"...
that's what the masses have all been told!!!
What about the muskets, Gatlings and Winchesters,
that permeated the colonial days of old?

"Weapons of Mass Destruction"...
can cripple and destroy a race!!!
Ask the Africans, Native Americans and Iraqis,
to solemnly state their cases.

Africa was invaded with muskets,
when her nations were throwing spears...
they heard *weapons of mass destruction,*
ringing *"slavery"* in their ears.

North America was invaded with Winchesters,
when her nations were shooting arrows...
they heard *weapons of mass destruction,*
communicating *"reservations"* and *"disaster"*.

Iraq was invaded with missiles,
when *"Saddam Hussein"* was spouting words...
they heard *weapons of mass destruction,*
killing *Sunnis, Shiites* and *Kurds*.

Cluster Bombs... Smart Bombs...
killing thousands upon thousands fast...
I feel a cold chill of desolation,
screaming out from centuries past.

Agent Orange... Anthrax...
oh, don't forget the *Serine Gas...*
all created with the deadly intent ...
of obliterating the human treasures of our past.

We are to denounce the winds of propaganda!
We are to discern the tenets of wrong from right!
We are to examine the spoils of war!
We should be guided by their plight!

Search out your *"spiritual light of conscience"*...
don't be misled by rumors, conjectures and fears;
perpetrated by the profiteers of war,
while the helpless poor are maimed and killed.

"Created and made in America",
scientific journals tell the truth!!!
Any weapon designed to kill in astronomical
numbers *"MASS DESTRUCTION"* is its use.

Any essential object, tool, commodity, or resource
can be used as a "weapon of mass destruction",
when placed solely in the hands of those whom
are bent on hatred, domination, and total control.

More people have been killed with guns that are
bought and sold every day, versus the nuclear bombs
that we have been told about and not seen...
Guns are indeed weapons of mass destruction!!!

~ Fight The Hype ~

"Ignore the hype that feeds the blight..."

On and on and on...
since we've been born;
witnessing Black degradation,
now our ethnic pride is gone.

Conditioned to respond,
in defense of other peoples fight;
We deny our ancestral obligations,
while absorbing the minutia and the hype.

African American lives are short,
though the roads to independence are long;
we must know and embrace our history,
in order to recover and carry on.

Ethnic focus should be the target,
for the extent of our years,
when we search out our collective path,
the vision will become clear.

Fight the hype!

One who spends his entire life
planting seeds in another man's field
will never reap a harvest of his own.

~ Don't Play It Again Sam... ~

Primitive drums beating in a New World,
sounds of urban chimes and symbols,
embracing little African American boys and girls.

And the music plays on...

Playing the *"Cry Baby Blues"* to a shallow beat,
while urban echoes and tremors rock the streets.
Show me more than 50%t two-parent families,
you will be given free lifetime food to eat.

And the music plays on...

Louder and louder the music plays...
Yet, millions of Black People have lost their way.
Glistening tunes of inadequacy caressing their faces;
Yes! Honor and dignity has lost its place.

And the music plays on...

Republican and Democratic rhetoric,
affirming the blues on down and out streets.
Promises of being pulled up by your bootstraps,
when you haven't socks or shoes on your feet.

And the music plays on...

Hey, Aunt Jemima...
Yo! Excuse me ma'am...
Can you give the drummer some...
Oh no, skip a beat... don't play it again Sam...

On and on and on, the "Cry Baby Blues" plays on...
until the bodies are dead and the corpses are gone!
Yet... the misery and self-degradation won't go away,
until the "enlightened generation" shows up to play...

~ Am-Bushed ~

Hear the drum beats of a New World...
the sagas and woes of elderly Americans,
baby boomers, teenage boys and girls.

Caught up in a trance, dancing a new dance.
Right to vote, no joke...
oops! recount... that's all she wrote!

Yes she… she as in Florida's Secretary Of State
and a conservative US Supreme Court…
Justice Clarence Thomas and his posy mobilized...
and that's all she wrote!

Political hand writing pontificating...
like ghostly hieroglyphics on a wall;
calling the shots, overturning history,
manipulating election results… damning us all!

That's all she wrote!

"Stay out of the Bushs...",
I heard the scream of a beacon's call;
if we forget civil rights and voters registration...
they will surely damn us all.

"George W. Bush Jr.... next president of America..."
the rigged Electoral College decried;
with the swing vote and no recount,
a propped up looser survives.

And worst of all my people,
"*morning time*" has come.
Reverend Jesse Jackson..., an adulterous child,
count the deal as done.

Think twice to recognize...

before eating the tainted fruit...
and just maybe you will awake
from the winds of propaganda
to know and embrace the truth.

That's all she wrote!!!

Our forefathers struggled and died,
to earn Negroes and Blacks the right to vote…
It's easy to stay home… only to complain later,
after being disenfranchised and having missed the boat.

We have a responsibility to exercise the privilege…
of voting our political values to remain free…
by engaging the political process that protects America
from becoming a "dictatorial democracy"!!!

~ Urban Warrior ~

"A tribute to Huey P. Newton "

Bewail a champion's cry,
beneath the euphoric calm;
echoing the relentless Black struggle,
resounding a hero's alarm.

Silenced by quest,
of past days undone;
adorned as a warrior,
by a murderous gun.

Huey our shield...
fashioned by social design;
resigned to the struggle,
of reshaping our time.

With the establishment you wrestled,
in defense of our fight;
for the achievement of balance,
in the struggle for human rights.

Huey oh so beautiful,
although misunderstood;
even by the brothers and sisters,
whom you sought to do good.

Sleep proud great Panther,
for your day of rest has come;
you need not wake tomorrow,
for your work is done.

We the awakened giants,
sure mourn for your touch;
you will forever be missed,
we love you so much.

Sleep on...
Great Panther...
Sleep on...

~ Huey P. Newton ~

~ 1942 thru 1989 ~

Founder of the Black Panther Party for Self-Defense at a time when white police officers were brutalizing and killing Black People with impunity, in many urban Black communities throughout America.

The Black Panther Party was birthed in Oakland, California in 1966 to defend the Black community against the blatant police violence and brutality that Blacks are experiencing throughout America today. *Yes... Black lives matter!!!*

"My fear was not of death itself, but a death without meaning. I wanted my death to be something the people could relate to, a basis for further mobilization of the community." {Revolutionary Suicide - page 179}

~ The GREATEST ~

Outside of the boxing ring,
he was an ambassador to millions…
Inside of the boxing ring,
he was an awesome wonder to behold…

A young kid from Louisville, Kentucky
born Cassius Marcellus Clay, Jr.,
confident, sassy, braggart, and bold.
Ali… Ali… Ali…

"Ain't I pretty?"

"Float like a butterfly…
Sting like a bee…
Your hands can't hit…
what your eyes can't see."

"I am the greatest!"

The Negro's Cassius Clay!
The Nation of Islam's Muhammad Ali!
One who forsook his world heavy weight crown
and risked imprisonment and his fortune to be free.

"I shook up the world!"

"I'm as pretty as a girl…
Lightning fast on my feet…
I'm too fast to be hit…
and can't possibly be beat."

"I'm a bad man!"

"I've turned the world upside down!
If you step in the ring with me,
not only will I whoop you…
but I'll predict in what round."

"I can't be beat"!

I've whooped...
Sonny Liston, George Foreman,
Joe Frazier and the *"United States Government"*
to name a few...

If you are fool enough
to step in the ring with me,
I'm gonna whoop you too.

"I must be The Greatest!"

~ *Tribute to Muhammad Ali* ~

*Ali was one of the most courageous African
Americans in the history of Black People to
brave either side of the Atlantic Ocean.*

*One who had the gifted ability to understand
that a people's history and experience is their truth...
a truth that is to be embraced and spoken of in truth.*

*Ali had the uncanny ability to take "difficult truth"
and use it as a carpenter's tool with skill to build,
rather than as a weapon of war to bludgeon and kill.*

*Muhammad Ali took "painful truth" and fashioned it
into a beautifully breath-taking paradox that became a
delicacy for all to feast upon and be incredibly filled.*

*Few men Black or White have measured up to Ali.
He was and is a role model and hero to many,
one who is extremely respected, loved and admired.*

*We honor your legacy of authenticity...
Muhammad Ali... The People's Champ!!!*

~ We Be Trying ~

"Historical trappings of Willie Lynch…"

In trouble times,
when ever than on my mind;
you no comfort me,
you pitch bitch all de time.

But I love you woman!
So I try..., *I try hard y'all!*
I work..., *I work hard y'all!*
I pray..., *I pray hard y'all!*

I put ever than on line...
to seek success,
I strive to find.

I be struggling,
no matter where I be;
but you no understand,
you turn your back on me.

But times change...
nothing stay same,
except true enemy.

Time be running out...
Baby wake up!

When viewing life through the lens of another,
we oftentimes see the enemy as being ourselves …

~ Society's New Breed ~

White girls high-stepping, on the prowl…
stalking, flirting, looking proud;
Prancing, sashaying, looking real good,
recruiting our "*MONEY-MAKERS*", distressing the hood.

Brothers openly checking them,
although culturally remanded;
White boys don't like it,
sisters definitely can't stand it.

Stepping tall, free and swaggered…
provocatively moving their sassy makers,
can't hardly wait for a brother to tap it,
so they can have some brown babies.

Vanilla bread leavened...
fermenting a batch of chocolate seeds...
blending a forbidden racial concoction,
producing "*Society's New Breed*".

A reversal of tradition,
society's fences all torn down;
Black and White... fusing,
into vanilla, yellow and brown.

A recipe from the first,
past down from slavery's birth;
like the "*Good Reverend*" once told me,
America is a "*Ethnic Bouquet of Roses*".

Females are the "wealth transfer agents"
in all major western societies.
Whatever the wife inherits from the husband
goes back to her own people not yours…
and we wonder while collectively we don't amass wealth!!!

~ African Queen ~

Smiling eyes...
secluded within a covert smile,
reflecting the heavens
of a latent desire.

You are an African woman!!!

You are kind... you are neat,
you are candid, you are sweet,
you are different, you are human,
you are individual.

You are a mannered woman
somewhat reserved and coy,
you kindle the strongest of men
from within the average boy.

You are an African woman!!!

You are unique... you are sober,
you are different from the rest,
you are one of a kind,
you are one of the best.

You are smart... you are private,
you wear a glow,
you have a lot to give,
and that I know.

When you embrace my world
my heart pounds and swells,
you are from a special design,
that I can tell.

You are impeccably beautiful,
you are deliciously sweet,

you are the picture of perfect,
you are totally complete.

You are a woman of women,
you are a lady without fail,
you are the essence of female,
you are at the top of the scale.

You are stylish and elegant,
you exemplify grace and poise,
you dazzle the world
with your womanly joy.

You are an African woman!!!

In order for one to truly be a king…
his queen must be his crown…
Our sisters are our "ethnic crowns"…
we are to love, honor, cherish and adore them…

~ A Strong Black Father ~

"In remembrance of my dad..."

Sixty Eight, that's great...
Thank God, Oh what a break...
It is through a strong father that I live today!
Thanks dad... you're special!

Now that I'm older...
remembering all you told me;
You taught me quite a lot,
I owe you all I've got.

You were truly a remarkable man,
having taken a positive stand;
You taught me how to plan,
in order to be a better man.

For all the days I live,
in your precious shadow...
I'll plan, I'll build.
Oh what a life worth living!

I thank God for your giving.
Unlike many I have a lot...
You were truly wonderful.
In you... I found the example!

Daddy you endured the tests,
in order for us to be better than second best.
You taught us to do more with less,
to overcome the rigors of success.

My father was the epitome of a real Black man,
when things were challenging and times were tough,

he took "character", "sacrifice" and "perseverance"
and made progress, history and a better life!

Through his positive example,
I have been blessed by God to walk in character
and make a difference in life as a man!

The presence of a "strong father figure" is essential
to how a young man is to properly behave and think.
Every developing boy needs one!

"Friendship"

This special acknowledgment is dedicated to my dear friend…

Charles E. Dickerson

Author and Publisher of…

From Kingdom to nigger-dom…

A People Lost In Translation!!!

An open book my friend…
you shared with us your open book,
the many names of Black folk,
you broke it down for us to see.

Reality of an open book…
Ethiopian, Negro, Black, nigger too,
African American… all burnt faces,
that was your pun.

Through it all…
the legacy is still there,
the truth sets us free…
what have we to fear?

Destiny of our people…
had a beginning though we all don't care,
the degradation that hurts,
makes some want to flee.

It makes some want to ignore
the existing catastrophe,
many others embrace the knowledge,
others fear.

As it quickens our inner man in despair…
often, we don't want to be reminded,
but truth reveals itself,
we are empowered.

Friendship and enlightenment…
like a precious diamond that has just been found,
we treasure and enjoy the beauty it displays…
shining, perfect illumination… an open book.

Your friendship, that is what it has meant to me.
A treasured jewel not kept in a box…
a diamond kept by the jeweler

and designed by God's own hands.

Like a true friend, a rare stone treasured...
continue to let your light shine,
because you are a rare diamond,
I only discovered through another friend of mine.

From the "Gifted Pen"
of a spirited poet, writer, and friend!

Patricia Ross Atkinson

~ A People's Ethnic Obligation ~

Our Fundamental Duties!!!

Our fundamental duties toward ourselves are to be about our *Heavenly Father's and earthly fathers' business.* Unfortunately, we cannot be about the business of either if we know nothing about our fathers. In the book of Luke chapter 2, verse 49 Jesus at 12 years of age stated the following to his parents..., *"Why did you seek me? Did you not know that I must be about my Father's business?"* Jesus could not have conducted His Father's business had He lacked the knowledge and understanding of His Father and the business at hand.

This principle applies to all people including ourselves, we must... (1) seek to know our Creator and put Him first in all things, (2) seek to know the truth about our forefathers and ourselves and practice that truth, (3) learn the truth about others and be guided by that knowledge *(good and bad)*, (4) teach our children and others the truth about who we are through positive example, (5) always strive to be the *"good human"* with the ultimate goal of *pleasing God!!!*

Re-education is the key to our cultural resurrection, which clears the path to reconstructing our *"native ethnicity". This is our earthly father's business!!!* We have a personal obligation of: (1) knowing who we are, (2) in relationship to where we are, (3) while sharing the understanding of what we as a people need to do individually and collectively to advance. The distinction between "EDUCATION" and "SOCIALIZATION" is critical. Thus far we have been socialized into believing that *"modern day education"* without *"native cultural enlightenment"* is the key to progress. History has shown that *"formal education"* without *"knowledge of self"* is not fruitful and effective for long-term growth and group prosperity.

By reading *"our own people books"* that are *"written in flesh"* and compiled in *"books of person"*, we avoid becoming mere bookends on humanities shelf of life, wherein entire nations and races of people are tragically reduced to the level of human ornaments and objects for social amusement. Unlike traditional books that are written in ink and printed on paper, *"books of person"* are *"spirit filled"*, *"action inscribed"*, *"ethnically charged"* diaries that are outlined from within the human collective and choreographed in flesh. These *"books of person"* represent untold stories of human sacrifice and individual accomplishments that have been documented in *"flesh"* and oftentimes written in *"blood"*. These so-called *"books of person"* exist in the form of human depositories that house the collective experiences that shape the *spiritual, moral, and social foundations* of a people. *"Books of person"* have existed in our mist since the beginning of time.

When in search of answers, Black People should read from their own *"Book of Life"* first, without relying solely upon information acquired from the *"physical books"* and *"people books"* of others. Every Black person is an important page in the ever expanding human encyclopedia known as the *"Black Experience"*, which is the oldest and greatest book of human endeavor in the history of human existence.

Our most skillful, courageous, and brilliant advocate, Malcolm X stated the following regarding history... *"Of all our studies, history is best qualified to reward our research"*. We have an obligation to study our history in order to understand the *"cultural and spiritual truth"* of our people, which will provide the critical knowledge required for *"each one to teach one"*!!!

~ Publisher's Note ~

On behalf of Neo-Nexus Publishing, LLC
I personally thank you for investing
your capital, time and energy
into the exploration of…

"From Kingdom… to nigger-dom"
"A People Lost In Translation!!!"

It is my sincere hope that this
long awaited publication measured up
to your literary expectation and satisfied
your historical interest and desire
…as a cultural seeker.

Charles E. Dickerson

~ Cultural Acknowledgement ~

"Munirah Uche Asha African Study Group"
~ "One Who Teaches Thought Life" ~
1980s thru 1990s - Columbia, SC
Sister Yvette Scott
Founder

"Voice of United Africa"
1980s thru 1990s - Alexandria, VA
Brother Carl Kpoto
"Citizen of Ghana"
Founder

www.ingramcontent.com/pod-product-compliance
Lightning Source LLC
Chambersburg PA
CBHW051957090426
42741CB00008B/1431

* 9 7 8 0 9 8 4 6 6 7 3 7 6 *